Buddha Śākyamuni

Guru Rinpoche

༄༅། །སློབ་དཔོན་ཆེན་པོ་པདྨ་འབྱུང་གནས་ཀྱིས་མཛད་པའི་ མན་ངག་ལྟ་བའི་ཕྲེང་བའི་རྩ་བ་དང་མཆན་འགྲེལ་ ནོར་བུའི་བང་མཛོད་ཅེས་བྱ་བ་བཞུགས། །

པདྨ་ཀཱ་རའི་སྒྲ་བསྒྱུར་མཐུན་ཚོགས་ནས་
སྒྲ་བསྒྱུར་ཞུས།།

A Garland of Views

A Guide to View, Meditation, and Result in the Nine Vehicles

Padmasambhava's classic text

with a commentary by

Jamgön Mipham

Translated by the Padmakara Translation Group

Shambhala
Boston & London
2015

Shambhala Publications, Inc.
Horticultural Hall
300 Massachusetts Avenue
Boston, Massachusetts 02115
www.shambhala.com

9 8 7 6 5 4 3 2 1

First Edition
Printed in the United States of America

♾ This edition is printed on acid-free paper that meets the American National Standards Institute z39.48 Standard.
♻ This book is printed on 30% postconsumer recycled paper.
For more information please visit www.shambhala.com.

Distributed in the United States by Penguin Random House LLC
and in Canada by Random House of Canada Ltd

Designed by Gopa & Ted2, Inc.

Library of Congress Cataloging-in-Publication Data
Padma Sambhava, approximately 717 to approximately 762, author.
A garland of views: a guide to view, meditation, and result in the nine vehicles: Padmasambhava's classic text with a commentary by Jamgön Mipham / Translated by the Padmakara Translation Group.—First edition.
pages cm.
Includes bibliographical references and index.
Translated from Tibetan.
ISBN 978-1-61180-296-2 (hardback)
1. Rñin-ma-pa (Sect)—Doctrines—Early works to 1800. I. Mi-pham-rgya-mtsho, 'Jam-mgon 'Ju, 1846–1912. II. Padma Sambhava, approximately 717 to approximately 762. Man ngag lta ba'i phreng ba. III. Padma Sambhava, approximately 717 to approximately 762. Man ngag lta ba'i phreng ba. English. IV. Comité de traduction Padmakara. V. Title.
BQ7950.P324M3613 2015
294.3'923—dc23
2015009884

The Padmakara Translation Group gratefully acknowledges the generous support of the Tsadra Foundation in sponsoring the translation and preparation of this book.

Contents

Topical Outline of *A Treasury of Gems*

- I. Introduction
  - A. Explanation of the title
  - B. Expression of veneration
- II. The main body of the text
  - A. Explanation of the different views
    - 1. Explanation of non-Buddhists' views
      - a. Brief introduction
      - b. Detailed explanation
        - i. Explanation of the unreflective and the materialists
        - ii. Explanation of the nihilistic extremists and eternalistic extremists
    - 2. Explanation of Buddhists' views
      - a. Brief introduction
      - b. Detailed explanation
        - i. Presentation of the vehicle of characteristics
          - A) Brief introduction
          - B) Detailed explanation
            - 1) Explanation of the Listener Vehicle
            - 2) Explanation of the Solitary Realizer Vehicle
            - 3) Explanation of the Bodhisattva Vehicle
        - ii. Presentation of the Mantra Vehicle
          - A) Brief introduction
          - B) Detailed explanation

1) Presentation of Kriyātantra
2) Presentation of Ubhayatantra
3) Presentation of Yogatantra
    a) Brief introduction
    b) Detailed explanation
        i) Presentation of the outer Yogatantra
        ii) Presentation of the inner Yogatantra
            (A) Brief introduction
            (B) Detailed explanation
                (1) A general explanation of the three methods
                    (a) The method of generation
                    (b) The method of perfection
                    (c) The method of the Great Perfection
                (2) A specific explanation of the avenues for applying the three methods
                    (a) The four kinds of realization
                    (b) The three characteristics
                    (c) The four branches
                    (d) The four stages of entering the maṇḍala

B. An explanation of the different kinds of yogic disciplines
    1. Brief introduction
    2. Detailed explanation

III. Conclusion
    A. The disciples for whom these instructions were intended
    B. Colophon marking the completion of the text

Foreword

The great Indian master Padmasambhava is considered to be an emanation of Buddha Shakyamuni, who predicted that he would be a great propagator of the tantric teachings in this world. He was instrumental, along with other great masters, in establishing the Buddha's teachings in Tibet in the eighth century. So preeminent was his influence that ever since he has been revered in the Land of Snows as Guru Rinpoche, the Precious Teacher.

While most of the numerous teachings that he gave during his stay in Tibet were hidden as treasure by his disciples, to be rediscovered later by their emanations in accordance with the Guru's predictions, this text is unusual in that it has come down to us through the oral lineage, passed on from master to disciple over the centuries. In it, Guru Rinpoche gives an account of the different views held by the various Buddhist schools and by non-Buddhists. If we wish to attain awakening or buddhahood, adopting the right view is crucial to the practice of the path, for as Mipham Rinpoche has pointed out, it is necessary for us to see properly if our feet are to take us in the right direction. It is by gaining a knowledge of the different views that we can know which views should be rejected and which views will most benefit us in our progress on the spiritual path that leads to our becoming a buddha.

Although an intellectual understanding of the view of the Middle Way, for example, one arrived at by employing analysis and debate, is certainly useful in serving as a basic foundation for establishing the correct view, Guru Rinpoche's intention in this text is not to provide us with a subject for academic discussion but rather to inspire us to practice the Buddhist path sincerely, with the aim of attaining buddhahood and benefiting all those whose erroneous views have led them into their present condition of obscuration and suffering.

I am very happy that the Padmakara Translation Group has made a new translation of this precious work available for English readers, along with the illuminating commentary of Mipham Rinpoche, and I hope that all who read it will find in it the inspiration necessary in order to progress in their spiritual practice, to become awakened as did all the buddhas in the past.

Jigme Khyentse Rinpoche

Translator's Introduction

From the time he first began to teach the Dharma, Buddha Śākyamuni recognized in his followers the very human need to order things into neat categories. In an age when the teachings were yet to be preserved in written form, the recording and broadcasting of the Buddha's word depended on his disciples' memories. For those who did not have the arhats' superhuman powers of retention, breaking the different subjects down into categories must have been a valuable aid. A tradition of enumeration and classification was thus established and was further developed and refined by the great Indian masters during the centuries that followed.

With the introduction of Buddhism into Tibet in the eighth century CE, an enormous volume of teachings was imported from India over a relatively short time. For the Tibetans trying to make sense of this flood of new ideas—more than a thousand years of accumulated literature, covering a large number of different lineages and schools of thought—the need to order and classify the subject matter must have been all the more imperative.

One area that concerned Tibetan scholars was the classification of the Buddhist teachings in terms of the different sorts of people who might practice them—in other words, how the teachings were to be divided into different approaches or vehicles. *A Garland of Views* holds a significant place in the development of this classification, for it was composed by the great Indian master Padmasambhava at the very moment that the Buddhist teachings were being established in Tibet. It provided the basis for the system of nine vehicles (three sūtra vehicles and six tantra vehicles) that subsequently became the accepted way of classifying the different Buddhist paths in the Nyingma School, whose teachings were based on the earlier, eighth-century translations. The system adopted by the followers of the New Translation schools, on the other hand, was based on the tantras brought to Tibet from India from the tenth century onward and employed a scheme of four tantra vehicles.[1]

In *A Garland of Views*, Padmasambhava compares the different vehicles on the basis of three criteria—view, meditation, and result. He devotes the final section of the text to a comparison using a fourth criterion—spiritual training and yogic discipline or conduct. Of all these, the view is of paramount importance. The way we look at the world decides the path we will take, whether spiritual or otherwise. When we see things erroneously, we create our own (and others') suffering, and if we are to change our condition, we need to make radical changes to our view of reality. Once the view has been established, we can meditate on it, training our minds by means of spiritual practice and tuning our activities through appropriate conduct, until we finally achieve the result. The particular view with which a person thus sets out on the spiritual path depends on his or her particular mental disposition. It is because individuals present such a variety of dispositions, with different degrees of ability and readiness to understand and accept certain views, that the Buddha and his spiritual heirs taught the different vehicles that are outlined in this text and described in order of the increasing subtlety and profundity of their corresponding views.

Padmasambhava's presentation of these vehicles is based on a few terse lines from the *Guhyagarbha-tantra*, cited by Mipham Rinpoche at the very beginning of his commentary. Indeed, the designation of *A Garland of Views* as a "pith instruction" is indicative of its belonging to one of the three genres of tantric literature—namely, tantras (Skt. *tantra*, Tib. *rgyud*), the source texts taught by the buddhas in this and other realms; explanatory teachings (*āgama* or *lung*), which expand on the subjects of their related tantras: and pith, or essential, instructions (*upadeśa* or *man ngag*), in which the complex and difficult ideas presented in the tantras and explanatory texts are essentialized in a way that facilitates their implementation. These three categories can also be associated in turn with the three inner yogas of the Nyingma tradition—Mahāyoga, Anuyoga, and Atiyoga, respectively.

A Garland of Views is thus a pith instruction related to the *Guhyagarbha-tantra* and is a presentation of its subject matter from the perspective of Atiyoga, or the Great Perfection. This is why most of the quotations used both in Padmasambhava's text and Mipham Rinpoche's commentary are taken from that tantra, a fact that explains the particular choice and use of terms as compared with other texts. Happily, certain of these differences, notably the names used to refer to the non-Buddhist schools, are painstakingly explained by Mipham. It should be noted, also, that although the *Guhyagarbha-tantra* is generally described by Nyingma scholars as the root tantra of the vehicle they now call Mahāyoga, some Indian masters in the eighth century considered it to be the main canonical source for Atiyoga. Indeed, Mipham refers to it as "the glory of all the tantras and explanatory teachings that show how all phenomena are, from the very beginning, spontaneously present as the Great Perfection."

It is thus worth bearing in mind the origins of *A Garland of Views* if one is to get the most out of this dense and difficult text. Beginners struggling to grasp its complex ideas should remember that, as the text's subtitle suggests, Padmasambhava intended it as a memory aid for disciples who were already familiar with both the theory and practice of the vehicles he describes. Even experienced readers may find themselves bewildered by his presentation, which reflects as much the particular thinking of the period as the content of the source tantra. And while Mipham Rinpoche's explanations provide much welcome detail, commentaries of this type, which belong to the genre known as "commentaries by annotation" (Tib. *mchan 'grel*), do not always offer the easiest approach to their subject. Although some works of this sort may have been deliberately prepared with a view to publication, many began life as a copy of an original treatise into which the author had inserted marginal notes. The notes could be based on oral explanations of the treatise or consist of appropriate passages copied from existing commentaries. The resulting annotated copy would have served the author's own personal use and perhaps as a series of lecture notes to be referred to when teaching. And, as seems to have been the case with the present commentary, it was sometimes only after their master's death that his disciples decided to turn his annotated copy into a publishable work, splicing the root text and the marginal notes together to form coherent prose. Apart from the provision of a structural outline (*sa bcad*) and clear section headings, there was little or no editing, for the master's words, by definition, were not to be improved on. It is hardly surprising, then, that commentaries by annotation, for all their handy conciseness, are in some ways less easy to understand than longer and more detailed commentaries. And it should be noted that in the traditional setting of the monastic colleges in Tibet, even the most accessible commentaries were rarely read without the full accompanying explanations of learned *khenpos*.

In this book, we have attempted to ease the reader's task with the provision of notes and a glossary. More detailed information on the Great Perfection and the nine vehicles should be sought from qualified teachers and from the relevant literature (see the bibliography at the end of the book). It is our hope that after repeated study of the Buddhist teachings, our readers will truly find in this translation the refreshment for their memories that Guru Padmasambhava intended and that they will be able to absorb the blessings of his words of truth, however much these may have been distorted and attenuated by our own very limited understanding of them.

The translation of this work would have been impossible without the generous advice and support of our teachers, in particular Pema Wangyal Rinpoche and Jigme Khyentse Rinpoche. We are also most grateful to Alak Zenkar Rinpoche and Khenpo Tenzin Norgay for the time they spent answering our questions. The main work of translating *A Garland of Views* was carried out by Stephen Gethin, who alone is responsible for any errors and misinterpretations. Invaluable help was received from other members of the Padmakara Translation Group: Wulstan Fletcher, who painstakingly read through the draft translation, and Helena Blankleder and John Canti, who made many useful suggestions. Larrie Gethin kindly read the final draft and pointed out a number of inconsistencies. Once again, we are indebted to Tsadra Foundation for its generous and patient sponsorship of this translation project. Finally, we are, as ever, grateful to Nikko Odiseos, Michael Wakoff, and the Shambhala team for their energy and expertise in producing the finished book.

A Garland of Views

A Pith Instruction by the Great Master Padmasambhava

༄༅། །མན་ངག་ལྟ་བའི་ཕྲེང་བ་ཞེས་བྱ་བ་བཞུགས་སོ།།

༄༅། །ལྟ་བ་དང་ཐེག་པ་ལ་སོགས་པའི་ཁྱད་པར་བསྡུས་པའི་བསྐྱུད་བྱང་།

བཅོམ་ལྡན་འདས་འཇམ་དཔལ་གཞོན་ནུ་དང་། རྡོ་རྗེ་ཆོས་ལ་ཕྱག་འཚལ་ལོ། །

འཇིག་རྟེན་གྱི་ཁམས་ན་སེམས་ཅན་ཕྱིན་ཅི་ལོག་གི་ལྟ་བ་གྲངས་མེད་པ་མདོ་རྣམ་པ་བཞིར་འདུས་ཏེ། ཕྱལ་བ་དང་། རྒྱང་འཕེན་དང་། མུར་ཐུག་དང་། མུ་སྟེགས་པའོ། །

དེ་ལ་ཕྱལ་བ་ནི་ཆོས་ཐམས་ཅད་རྒྱུ་དང་འབྲས་བུ་ཡོད་མེད་དུ་མ་རྟོགས་ཏེ། ཀུན་ཏུ་རྨོངས་པའོ། །

རྒྱང་འཕེན་ནི་ཚེ་སྔ་ཕྱི་ཡོད་མེད་དུ་མ་རྟོགས་ཤིང་། ཚེ་གཅིག་ལ་བཙན་ཕྱུག་དང་མཐུ་སྟོབས་སྒྲུབ་པ་སྟེ། འཇིག་རྟེན་གྱི་གསང་ཚིག་ལ་བརྟེན་པའོ། །

མུར་ཐུག་པ་ནི། ཆོས་ཐམས་ཅད་རྒྱུ་དང་འབྲས་བུ་མེད་པ་སྟེ། ཚེ་གཅིག་ལ་སྐྱེས་པའི་ཆོས་ཐམས་ཅད་གློ་བུར་དུ་སྐྱེས་ལ་མཐའ་ཆད་པར་ལྟ་བའོ། །

མུ་སྟེགས་པ་ནི་ཆོས་ཐམས་ཅད་ལ་ཀུན་ཏུ་བརྟགས་པས་བདག་རྟག་པ་ཞིག་ཡོད་པར་ལྟ་བ་སྟེ། དེ་ལ་ཡང་རྒྱུ་མེད་ལ་འབྲས་བུ་ཡོད་པར་ལྟ་བ་དང་། རྒྱུ་འབྲས་ལོག་པར་ལྟ་བ་དང་། རྒྱུ་ཡོད་པ་ལ་འབྲས་བུ་མེད་པར་ལྟ་བ་དང་། །

འདི་དག་ནི་མ་རིག་པའི་ལྟ་བའོ། །

A memory aid summarizing the distinctive features of the views and vehicles.

I pay homage to the Lord Mañjuśrī the youthful, and to Vajradharma.

The false views entertained by beings in the world are without number, but they can be summarized as being of four kinds: those of the unreflective, the materialists, the nihilistic extremists, and the eternalistic extremists.

The unreflective have no understanding as to whether or not phenomena are the causes or results of anything. They are completely confused.

The materialists have no understanding as to whether or not there are previous and future lives. They work to achieve strength, riches, and power in this one life, for which they rely on the secret knowledge of worldly beings.

Nihilistic extremists do not believe that things have causes and effects. For them, everything that comes about in this one life does so "just like that" and finally is extinguished.

Eternalistic extremists believe in a permanent self, which they imagine to be present in all phenomena. Some believe in a reality—an effect—for which there is no cause. Some have an incorrect view of causality. Some believe that whereas the cause is real, the effects are unreal.

All these are the views of ignorance.

འཇིག་རྟེན་ལས་འདས་པའི་ལམ་ལ་ཡང་རྣམ་པ་གཉིས་ཏེ། མཚན་ཉིད་ཀྱི་ཐེག་པ་དང་རྡོ་རྗེའི་ཐེག་པའོ། །

མཚན་ཉིད་ཀྱི་ཐེག་པ་ལ་ཡང་རྣམ་པ་གསུམ་སྟེ་ཉན་ཐོས་ཀྱི་ཐེག་པ་དང་། རང་སངས་རྒྱས་ཀྱི་ཐེག་པ་དང་། བྱང་ཆུབ་སེམས་དཔའི་ཐེག་པའོ། །

དེ་ལ་ཉན་ཐོས་ཀྱི་ཐེག་པ་ལ་ཞུགས་པ་རྣམས་ཀྱི་ལྟ་བ་ནི། ཆོས་ཐམས་ཅད་ལ་མུ་སྟེགས་པ་ལ་སོགས་པས་སྒྲོ་དང་སྐུར་བས་ཀུན་ཏུ་བརྟགས་པས། ཡེ་མེད་པ་ཆད་པའི་ལྟ་བ་དང་། རྟག་པ་ལ་སོགས་པའི་ཡོད་པར་ལྟ་བ་ནི། ཐག་པ་ལ་སྦྲུལ་དུ་མཐོང་བ་བཞིན་དུ་མེད་དེ། ཕུང་པོ་ཁམས་དང་སྐྱེ་མཆེད་ལ་སོགས་པའི་འབྱུང་བ་ཆེན་པོ་བཞིའི་རྡུལ་ཕྲ་རབ་དང་། རྣམ་པར་ཤེས་པ་ནི་དོན་དམ་པར་ཡོད་པར་ལྟ་ཞིང་། འཕགས་པའི་བདེན་པ་བཞི་བསྒོམས་པས་རིམ་གྱིས་འབྲས་བུ་རྣམ་པ་བཞི་འགྲུབ་པ་ཡིན་ནོ། །

རང་སངས་རྒྱས་ཀྱི་ཐེག་པ་ལ་ཞུགས་པ་རྣམས་ཀྱི་ལྟ་བ་ནི། ཆོས་ཐམས་ཅད་ལ་མུ་སྟེགས་ལ་སོགས་པས་སྒྲོ་དང་སྐུར་པས་ཀུན་ཏུ་བརྟག་པའི་བདག་རྟག་པ་ལ་སོགས་པ་མེད་པར་ལྟ་བ་ཉན་ཐོས་དང་མཐུན། དེ་ལས་ཁྱད་པར་དུ་གཟུགས་ཀྱི་ཕུང་པོའི་ཆོས་ཀྱི་ཕྱོགས་གཅིག་ལ་བདག་མེད་པར་རྟོགས་ཤིང་། རང་བྱང་ཆུབ་ཀྱི་འབྲས་བུ་འཐོབ་པའི་དུས་ནའང་། ཉན་ཐོས་ལྟར་དགེ་བའི་བཤེས་གཉེན་ལ་མི་ལྟོས་པར་སྔོན་གོམས་པའི་ཤུགས་ཀྱིས་རྟེན་ཅིང་འབྲེལ་བར་འབྱུང་བ་ཡན་ལག་བཅུ་གཉིས་ཀྱི་སྒོ་ནས་ཆོས་ཉིད་ཟབ་མོའི་དོན་རྟོགས་ནས། རང་བྱང་ཆུབ་ཀྱི་འབྲས་བུ་ཐོབ་པ་ཡིན་ནོ།།

༄ བྱང་ཆུབ་སེམས་དཔའི་ཐེག་པ་ལ་ཞུགས་པ་རྣམས་ཀྱི་ལྟ་བ་ནི།

The path that leads beyond the world has two aspects: the vehicle of characteristics and the Diamond Vehicle.

The vehicle of characteristics has three further divisions: the Listener Vehicle, the Solitary Realizer Vehicle, and the Bodhisattva Vehicle.

The followers of the Listener Vehicle believe that the views of the eternalistic extremists and so on amount to conceptual exaggerations and depreciations of phenomena as a whole. They thus consider that the nihilistic view that things have never existed and the eternalist view that they exist permanently and so on are as invalid as the belief that a rope is a snake. They consider that the infinitesimal particles of the four great elements that make up the aggregates, elements, senses-and-fields, and so forth, and also the instants of consciousness, exist on the ultimate level. By meditating on the Four Noble Truths, they progressively accomplish the four results.

Those engaged in the Solitary Realizer Vehicle agree with the listeners in denying the permanent self and so forth imagined by the eternalistic extremists and others, with their conceptual exaggerations and depreciations of the whole of phenomena. But they differ from them in that they have partially realized the absence of self in phenomena related to the aggregate of form. And unlike the listeners, when they attain the result (enlightenment as solitary realizers), they do so without relying on a spiritual teacher. It is, rather, by the force of previous habituation that they realize the profound ultimate nature of phenomena in terms of the twelve links of dependent arising and subsequently attain the result: the solitary realizers' enlightenment.

The view of those engaged in the Bodhisattva Vehicle is that,

ཀུན་ནས་ཉོན་མོངས་པ་དང་རྣམ་པར་བྱང་བའི་ཆོས་ཐམས་ཅད་དོན་དམ་པར་ནི་རང་བཞིན་མེད་པ་ཡིན་ལ། ཀུན་རྫོབ་ཏུ་ནི་སྒྱུ་མ་ཙམ་དུ་སོ་སོའི་མཚན་ཉིད་མ་འདྲེས་པར་ཡོད་དེ། ཕ་རོལ་ཏུ་ཕྱིན་པ་བཅུ་སྤྱད་པའི་འབྲས་བུ་ས་བཅུ་རིམ་གྱིས་བགྲོད་པའི་མཐར་བླ་ན་མེད་པའི་བྱང་ཆུབ་ཏུ་འགྲུབ་པར་འདོད་པ་ཡིན་ནོ།།

༄ རྡོ་རྗེ་ཐེག་པ་ལ་ཡང་རྣམ་པ་གསུམ་སྟེ། བྱ་བའི་རྒྱུད་ཀྱི་ཐེག་པ་དང་། གཉིས་ཀ་རྒྱུད་ཀྱི་ཐེག་པ་དང་། རྣལ་འབྱོར་གྱི་ཐེག་པའོ། །

དེ་ལ་བྱ་བའི་རྒྱུད་ཀྱི་ཐེག་པ་ལ་ཞུགས་པ་རྣམས་ཀྱི་ལྟ་བ་ནི། དོན་དམ་པར་སྐྱེ་འགག་མེད་པ་ལས། ཀུན་རྫོབ་ཏུ་ལྷའི་གཟུགས་ཀྱི་སྐུར་སྒོམ་ཞིང་སྐུའི་གཟུགས་བརྙན་དང་། ཐུགས་མཚན་དང་། བཟླས་བརྗོད་དང་། གཙང་སྦྲ་དང་། དུས་ཚིག་དང་། གཟའ་དང་། རྒྱུ་སྐར་ལ་སོགས་པ་གཙོ་བོར་ཡོ་བྱད་དང་རྒྱུ་རྐྱེན་ཚོགས་པའི་མཐུ་ལས་འགྲུབ་པའོ།།

༄ གཉིས་ཀ་རྒྱུད་ཀྱི་ཐེག་པ་ལ་ཞུགས་པ་རྣམས་ཀྱི་ལྟ་བ་ནི། དོན་དམ་པར་སྐྱེ་འགག་མེད་པ་ལས། ཀུན་རྫོབ་ཏུ་ལྷའི་གཟུགས་ཀྱི་སྐུ་བསྒོམ་ཞིང་། དེ་ཉིད་རྣམ་པ་བཞི་དང་ལྡན་པར་སྒོམ་པའི་ཏིང་ངེ་འཛིན་དང་། ཡོ་བྱད་དང་རྒྱུ་རྐྱེན་ལ་སོགས་པ་གཉིས་ཀ་ལ་བརྟེན་པ་ལས་འགྲུབ་པའོ།།

༄ རྣལ་འབྱོར་རྒྱུད་ཀྱི་ཐེག་པ་ལ་ཞུགས་པ་རྣམས་ཀྱི་ལྟ་བ་ནི་རྣམ་པ་གཉིས་ཏེ། རྣལ་འབྱོར་ཕྱི་པ་ཐུབ་པའི་རྒྱུད་ཀྱི་ཐེག་པ་དང་། རྣལ་འབྱོར་ནང་པ་ཐབས་ཀྱི་རྒྱུད་ཀྱི་ཐེག་པའོ། །

དེ་ལ་རྣལ་འབྱོར་ཕྱི་པ་ཐུབ་པའི་རྒྱུད་ཀྱི་ཐེག་པ་ལ་ཞུགས་པ་རྣམས་ཀྱི་ལྟ་བ་ནི།

on the ultimate level, all phenomena, whether of total affliction or of complete purity, are devoid of inherent existence, while on the relative level, they are mere illusions, each with its own distinct characteristics. As a result of their training in the ten transcendent perfections, bodhisattvas proceed in stages through the ten levels, at the end of which, they attain unsurpassable enlightenment.

The Diamond Vehicle is also divided into three: the vehicle of Kriyātantra, the vehicle of Ubhayatantra, and the vehicle of Yogatantra.

The view of those engaged in the vehicle of Kriyātantra is that, on the ultimate level, there is no arising or cessation. On this basis, they meditate, on the relative level, on the form body of the deity. By the power of bringing together the image of the deity's body, the implements symbolizing the deity's mind, the recitation of the mantra, and the requisite elements (above all, the observance of cleanliness, particular moments in time, the planets, constellations, and so forth), along with the cause and conditions, accomplishment is gained.

The view of those engaged in the vehicle of Ubhayatantra is that, on the ultimate level, there is no arising or cessation. On this basis, they meditate, on the relative level, on the form body of the deity. By relying on both meditative concentration endowed with four principles and all the other requisite elements, causes, and conditions, they gain accomplishment.

The view of those engaged in the vehicle of Yogatantra has two aspects—the vehicle of the outer Yogatantra of austerities and the vehicle of the inner Yogatantra of skillful means.

The view of those engaged in the vehicle of the outer Yogatantra

ཕྱི་ཡོ་བྱད་ལ་གཙོ་བོར་མི་འཛིན་པར་དོན་དམ་པ་སྐྱེ་འགགས་མེད་པའི་ལྷ་དང་ལྷ་མོ་དང་། དེ་དང་འདྲ་བའི་རྒྱུད་ཡོངས་སུ་དག་པའི་ཏིང་ངེ་འཛིན་གྱིས་འཕགས་པའི་གཟུགས་ཀྱི་སྐུ་ཕྱག་རྒྱ་བཞི་ལྡན་པར་བསྒོམས་པའི་རྣལ་འབྱོར་གཙོ་བོར་བྱས་པ་ལས་གྲུབ་པའོ། །

རྣལ་འབྱོར་ནང་པ་ཐབས་ཀྱི་རྒྱུད་ཀྱི་ཐེག་པ་ལ་ཞུགས་པ་རྣམས་ཀྱི་ལྟ་བ་ནི་རྣམ་པ་གསུམ་སྟེ། བསྐྱེད་པའི་ཚུལ་དང་། རྫོགས་པའི་ཚུལ་དང་། རྫོགས་པ་ཆེན་པོའི་ཚུལ་ལོ། །

དེ་ལ་བསྐྱེད་པའི་ཚུལ་ནི་ཏིང་ངེ་འཛིན་རྣམ་པ་གསུམ་རིམ་གྱིས་བསྐྱེད་དེ་དཀྱིལ་འཁོར་རིམ་གྱིས་བཀོད་ཅིང་བསྒོམ་པས་འགྲུབ་པའོ། །

རྫོགས་པའི་ཚུལ་ནི་དོན་དམ་པར་སྐྱེ་འགགས་མེད་པའི་ལྷ་དང་ལྷ་མོ་དང་། རྣམ་པར་མི་རྟོག་པའི་དོན་དབུ་མ་ཆོས་ཀྱི་དབྱིངས་ལས་ཀྱང་མ་གཡོས་ལ། ཀུན་རྫོབ་ཏུ་འཕགས་པའི་གཟུགས་ཀྱི་སྐུ་ཡང་གསལ་བར་བསྒོམས་ཞིང་མཉམ་ལ་མ་འདྲེས་པར་བསྒོམ་པས་འགྲུབ་བོ།།

༄ རྫོགས་པ་ཆེན་པོའི་ཚུལ་ནི། འཇིག་རྟེན་དང་འཇིག་རྟེན་ལས་འདས་པའི་ཆོས་ཐམས་ཅད་དབྱེར་མེད་པར་སྐུ་གསུང་ཐུགས་ཀྱི་དཀྱིལ་འཁོར་གྱི་རང་བཞིན་ཡེ་ནས་ཡིན་པར་རྟོགས་ནས་སྒོམ་པ་སྟེ། དེ་ཡང་རྒྱུད་ལས།

རྡོ་རྗེ་ཕུང་པོའི་ཡན་ལག་ནི། །
རྫོགས་པའི་སངས་རྒྱས་ལྔ་རུ་གྲགས། །

of austerities is as follows. Rather than emphasizing the outer requisites, they consider the yogic practice to be most important: they meditate on the male and female deities, who on the ultimate level are beyond arising and cessation; and with the concentration of a perfectly pure mind concordant with that view, they meditate, sealed with the four *mudrās*, on the form body of the sublime deity. By this means they gain accomplishment.

The view of those engaged in the vehicle of the inner Yogatantra of skillful means has three aspects: the method of generation, the method of perfection, and the method of the Great Perfection.

In the method of generation, the three concentrations are gradually developed and the maṇḍala is constructed step by step. By meditating in this way, accomplishment is gained.

In the method of perfection, on the ultimate level, one never moves from the male and female deities (who on the ultimate level are beyond arising and cessation) and from the expanse of truth, the middle way beyond all concepts. On the relative level, one clearly visualizes the form body of the sublime deity, meditating on everything as the same yet distinct. By this means, one gains accomplishment.

In the method of the Great Perfection, one realizes that all phenomena, mundane and supramundane, are inseparable in being, by nature and from the very beginning, the maṇḍala of the enlightened body, speech, and mind. One then meditates on this.

As it is said in the tantra:

> The vajra aggregates
> Are known as the five perfect buddhas.

སྐྱེ་མཆེད་ཁམས་རྣམས་མང་པོ་ཀུན། །
བྱང་ཆུབ་སེམས་དཔའི་དཀྱིལ་འཁོར་ཉིད། །
ས་ཆུ་སྤྱན་དང་མཱ་མ་ཀི །
མེ་རླུང་གོས་དཀར་སྒྲོལ་མ་སྟེ། །
ནམ་མཁའ་དབྱིངས་ཀྱི་དབང་ཕྱུག་མ། །
སྲིད་གསུམ་ཡེ་ནས་རྣམ་པར་དག །ཅེས་འབྱུང་སྟེ། །

འཁོར་བ་དང་མྱ་ངན་ལས་འདས་པའི་ཆོས་ཐམས་ཅད་ཡེ་ནས་མ་སྐྱེས་ལ། བྱ་བ་བྱེད་ནུས་པའི་སྒྱུ་མ་བདེ་བར་གཤེགས་པ་ཡབ་ཡུམ་བཅུ་ལ་སོགས་པའི་རང་བཞིན་ཡེ་ནས་ཡིན་པའི་ཕྱིར། །

ཆོས་ཐམས་ཅད་རང་བཞིན་གྱི་མྱ་ངན་ལས་འདས་པ་སྟེ། ཆེན་པོ་ལྔ་ནི་ཡུམ་ལྔའི་རང་བཞིན། ཕུང་པོ་ལྔ་ནི་རིགས་ལྔའི་སངས་རྒྱས། རྣམ་པར་ཤེས་པ་བཞི་ནི་བྱང་ཆུབ་སེམས་དཔའ་བཞིའི་རང་བཞིན། ཡུལ་བཞི་ནི་མཛེས་པའི་ལྷ་མོ་བཞིའི་རང་བཞིན། དབང་པོ་བཞི་ནི་བྱང་ཆུབ་སེམས་དཔའ་བཞིའི་རང་བཞིན། དུས་བཞི་ནི་མཆོད་པའི་ལྷ་མོ་བཞིའི་རང་བཞིན། །

ལུས་ཀྱི་དབང་པོ་དང་རྣམ་པར་ཤེས་པ་དང་། ཡུལ་དང་དེ་ལས་བྱུང་བའི་བྱང་ཆུབ་ཀྱི་སེམས་ནི། ཁྲོ་བོ་བཞིའི་རང་བཞིན། རྟག་ཆད་མུ་བཞི་ནི་ཁྲོ་མོ་བཞིའི་རང་བཞིན། ཡིད་ཀྱི་རྣམ་པར་ཤེས་པ་ནི་བྱང་ཆུབ་ཀྱི་སེམས་རྡོ་རྗེ་ཀུན་ཏུ་བཟང་པོའི་རང་བཞིན། ཡུལ་ཆོས་འདུས་བྱས་དང་འདུས་མ་བྱས་ནི། ཆོས་བྱ་བ་མོ་ཀུན་ཏུ་བཟང་མོའི་རང་བཞིན་ཏེ། །

དེ་དག་ཀྱང་ཡེ་ནས་མངོན་པར་རྫོགས་པར་སངས་རྒྱས་པའི་རང་བཞིན་ཡིན་གྱི། དེ་ལམ་གྱིས་སྒྲུབ་པ་མ་ཡིན་ནོ། །

All the many senses-and-fields
Are the maṇḍala of bodhisattvas.
Earth is Locanā, water Māmakī,
Fire is Pāṅḍaravāsinī, wind is Tārā,
And space Dhātvīśvarī.
The three worlds are pure from the beginning.

The phenomena of saṃsāra and nirvāṇa are unborn from the beginning, yet they appear in the manner of illusions, capable of functioning, and having the nature, since the beginning, of the ten male and female buddhas and so on.

All phenomena, therefore, are, by nature, the state of nirvāṇa. The five great elements are, by nature, the five female buddhas. The five aggregates are the buddhas of the five families. The four kinds of consciousnesses are, by nature, four bodhisattvas, and their four objects are, by nature, four beautiful goddesses. The four sense powers are, by nature, four bodhisattvas, and the four times are, by nature, four offering goddesses.

The organ of physical sensation, its related consciousness, its object, and the bodhicitta that arises from them are, by nature, four male wrathful deities. The four extreme views of eternalism, nihilism, and the rest are the four female wrathful deities. The mental consciousness, the adamantine bodhicitta, is, by nature, Samantabhadra. Its objects, phenomena both compounded and uncompounded, are, by nature, Samantabhadrī, matrix of all phenomena.

All the things just mentioned have primordially the nature of perfect, manifest buddha. This is not something newly accomplished through the practice of the path.

དེ་ལྟར་ཕྱོགས་བཅུ་དུས་གསུམ་དང་། ཁམས་གསུམ་ལ་སོགས་པ་འདུས་བྱས་དང་འདུས་མ་བྱས་པའི་ཆོས་ཐམས་ཅད་རང་གི་སེམས་ལས་གུད་ན་མེད་དེ། ཇི་སྐད་དུ།

རང་སེམས་སོ་སོར་རྟོག་པ་ནི། །
སངས་རྒྱས་བྱང་ཆུབ་དེ་ཉིད་དོ། །
འཇིག་རྟེན་གསུམ་པོ་དེ་ཉིད་དོ། །
འབྱུང་བ་ཆེ་རྣམས་དེ་ཉིད་དོ། །ཞེས་འབྱུང་ངོ་། །

ཇི་སྐད་དུ། །

ཆོས་རྣམས་ཐམས་ཅད་ནི་སེམས་ལ་གནས་སོ། །
སེམས་ནི་ནམ་མཁའ་ལ་གནས་སོ། །
ནམ་མཁའ་ནི་ཅི་ལ་ཡང་མི་གནས་སོ། །ཞེས་འབྱུང་བ་དང་། །
ཆོས་ཐམས་ཅད་ནི་ངོ་བོ་ཉིད་ཀྱིས་སྟོང་པའོ། །
ཆོས་ཐམས་ཅད་ནི་གདོད་མ་ནས་རྣམ་པར་དག་པའོ། །
ཆོས་ཐམས་ཅད་ནི་ཡོངས་ཀྱི་འོད་གསལ་བའོ། །
ཆོས་ཐམས་ཅད་ནི་རང་བཞིན་གྱིས་མྱ་ངན་ལས་འདས་པའོ། །
ཆོས་ཐམས་ཅད་ནི་མངོན་པར་རྫོགས་པར་སངས་རྒྱས་པའོ། །ཞེས་གསུངས་སོ། །

འདི་ནི་རྫོགས་པ་ཆེན་པོའོ། །

རྫོགས་པ་ཆེན་པོའི་ཚུལ་དེ་ནི། དེ་ལ་རྫོགས་པ་ཆེན་པོའི་ཚུལ་ནི། བསོད་ནམས་དང་ཡེ་ཤེས་ཀྱི་ཚོགས་རྫོགས་པ།

Thus, there are no phenomena, whether compounded or uncompounded (the ten directions, the three times, the three worlds, and so on), that exist separately from one's own mind. As it is said:

> Discerning consciousness, our mind,
> Is just the buddhas and the bodhisattvas.
> The three worlds are simply this.
> The great elements are simply this.

And:

> All phenomena abide within the mind.
> The mind abides in space.
> And space itself has no abode.

And:

> All phenomena are by their nature empty.
> All phenomena are primordially perfectly pure.
> All phenomena are completely radiant.
> All phenomena are, by nature, nirvāṇa.
> All phenomena are the perfect, manifest state of enlightenment.

Such is the Great Perfection.

The method of the Great Perfection (marginal note: "great" in the qualities of the result being spontaneously present and in the

འབྲས་བུའི་ཆོས་ལྡན་གྱིས་གྲུབ་པའི། ཚུལ་འདི་ནི་དོན་ལ་འཇུག་པའོ། །

རྟོགས་པ་རྣམ་བཞིའི་ལམ་གྱིས་ཡིད་ཆེས་ཏེ། རྟོགས་པ་རྣམ་པ་བཞི་ནི། རྒྱུ་གཅིག་པར་རྟོགས་པ་དང་། ཡིག་འབྲུའི་ཚུལ་གྱིས་རྟོགས་པ་དང་། བྱིན་གྱིས་རློབས་ཀྱིས་རྟོགས་པ་དང་། མངོན་སུམ་པར་རྟོགས་པའོ། །

དེ་ལ་རྒྱུ་གཅིག་པར་རྟོགས་པ་ནི། ཆོས་ཐམས་ཅད་དོན་དམ་པར་མ་སྐྱེས་པས་སོ་སོ་མ་ཡིན་པ་དང་། ཀུན་རྫོབ་ཏུ་སྒྱུ་མའི་མཚན་ཉིད་དུ་སོ་སོ་མ་ཡིན་པ་དང་། མ་སྐྱེས་པ་ཉིད་ཆུ་ཟླ་ལྟར་སྒྱུ་མ་སྣ་ཚོགས་སུ་སྣང་ཞིང་བྱ་བ་བྱེད་ནུས་པ་དང་། སྒྱུ་མ་ཉིད་ངོ་བོ་མེད་དེ་མ་སྐྱེས་པས་ཀུན་རྫོབ་དང་དོན་དམ་པར་དབྱེར་མེད་པས་རྒྱུ་གཅིག་པར་རྟོགས་པའོ། །

ཡིག་འབྲུའི་ཚུལ་གྱིས་རྟོགས་པ་ནི། ཆོས་ཐམས་ཅད་མ་སྐྱེས་པ་ནི་ཨ་སྟེ་གསུང་གི་རང་བཞིན། མ་སྐྱེས་པ་ཉིད་སྒྱུ་མར་སྣང་ཞིང་བྱ་བ་བྱེད་ནུས་པ་ནི་ཨོ་སྟེ་སྐུའི་རང་བཞིན། དེ་ལྟར་རྟོགས་པའི་རིག་པ་སྒྱུ་མའི་ཡེ་ཤེས་མཐའ་དབུས་མེད་པ་ནི་ཨོཾ་སྟེ་ཐུགས་ཀྱི་རང་བཞིན་དུ་རྟོགས་པའོ། །

བྱིན་གྱིས་བརླབས་ཀྱིས་རྟོགས་པ་ནི་དཔེར་ན་རས་དཀར་པོ་ལ་དམར་པོས་བྱིན་གྱིས་རློབ་པའི་མཐུ་བཙོད་ལ་ཡོད་པ་བཞིན་དུ། ཆོས་ཐམས་ཅད་སངས་རྒྱས་པར་བྱིན་གྱིས་རློབས་པའི་མཐུ་ཡང་། རྒྱུ་གཅིག་པ་དང་ཡིག་འབྲུའི་ཚུལ་གྱིས་མཐུ་བྱིན་གྱིས་རློབ་པར་རྟོགས་པའོ། །

method for entering that, and "perfection" in that the accumulations of merit and wisdom are perfect and complete) is as follows.

It is thanks to the path of the four kinds of realization that conviction is gained. The four kinds of realization are (1) the realization that there is a single cause, (2) realization by means of syllables, (3) realization through blessing, and (4) direct realization.

First, there is the realization that there is a single cause. Because, on the ultimate level, phenomena are unborn, they are not different from each other. Neither, on the relative level, are they distinct from each other in that they all have the character of illusion. That which is unborn appears in various kinds of displays, as illusory as the moon reflected in water, yet capable of performing functions. These illusions are devoid of essential nature; they are unborn. Thus, the relative and the ultimate are inseparable. This is the realization that there is a single cause.

Then follows the realization by means of syllables. The unborn nature of phenomena is symbolized by A, the nature of enlightened speech. This unborn nature appears as an illusory display, capable of performing functions and symbolized by O, the nature of the enlightened body. The awareness that realizes this—namely, the illusory gnosis, which is without center or circumference—is symbolized by OM, the nature of the enlightened mind. This is the realization by means of syllables.

The realization that comes about through blessing is the realization that just as the power to "bless" white cotton and make it red is present in madder, so too the power to bless all phenomena as enlightened lies in being blessed by the power of the realization that there is a single cause and of the realization by means of syllables.

མངོན་སུམ་པར་རྟོགས་པ་ནི། ཆོས་ཐམས་ཅད་ཡེ་ནས་སངས་རྒྱས་པར་གནས་པ་དེ་ཡང་ལུང་དང་མན་ངག་དང་འགལ་བ་ཡང་མ་ཡིན་ལ། ལུང་དང་མན་ངག་གི་ཚིག་ཙམ་ལ་བརྟེན་པ་ཡང་མ་ཡིན་པར། རང་གི་རིག་པས་བློའི་གཏིང་དུ་ཡིད་ཆེས་པས་མངོན་སུམ་དུ་རྟོགས་པའོ། །

ལམ་གྱི་ཡིད་ཆེས་པ་ནི། རྟོགས་པ་རྣམ་པ་བཞིའི་དོན་རིག་པ་ཉིད་རྣལ་འབྱོར་པའི་ལམ་སྟེ། དེ་ཡང་རྒྱུ་བསྒྲུབ་པའི་འབྲས་བུ་འབྱུང་བའི་དུས་ལ་ལྟོས་པ་ལྟ་བུ་མ་ཡིན་གྱི། རང་གིས་མངོན་སུམ་དུ་རྟོགས་ཤིང་ཡིད་ཆེས་པའོ། །

དེ་ལ་མཚན་ཉིད་གསུམ་གྱིས་དོན་མཐར་ཕྱིན་པར་འགྱུར་ཏེ། རྟོགས་པ་རྣམ་པ་བཞིའི་ཚུལ་རིག་པ་ནི་ཤེས་པའི་མཚན་ཉིད་དོ། །ཡང་ནས་ཡང་དུ་གོམས་པར་བྱེད་པ་ནི་འཇུག་པའི་མཚན་ཉིད་དོ། །གོམས་པའི་མཐུས་མངོན་དུ་གྱུར་པ་ནི་འབྲས་བུའི་མཚན་ཉིད་དོ། །མཚན་ཉིད་གསུམ་གྱིས་འབྲེལ་པ་དང་། དགོས་པ་དང་། དགོས་པའི་ཡང་དགོས་པ་སྟོན་ཏེ། །

དེ་ལ་འབྲེལ་པ་ནི། ཀུན་ནས་ཉོན་མོངས་པ་དང་། རྣམ་པར་བྱང་བའི་ཆོས་སུ་བཏགས་པ་ཐམས་ཅད། ཡེ་ནས་སྐུ་གསུང་ཐུགས་ཀྱི་བདག་ཉིད། རང་བཞིན་གྱིས་སངས་རྒྱས་པའི་དབྱིངས་དང་། བྱིན་རླབས་པའི་དོན་རྟོགས་པ་ནི། རྒྱུ་ཤེས་པའི་མཚན་ཉིད་དེ། དེ་ནི་བླ་ན་མེད་པའི་སངས་རྒྱས་སུ་གྲུབ་པའི་རྒྱུ་ཡིན་པའི་དོན་དུ་འབྲེལ་བའོ། །

དགོས་པ་ནི་ཀུན་ནས་ཉོན་མོངས་པ་དང་། རྣམ་པར་བྱང་བའི་ཆོས་དང་། སྨན་ལྔ་དང་།

Finally, there is direct realization through perception. The fact that phenomena abide primordially in the enlightened state does not contradict the scriptures and pith instructions. On the other hand, it is not by relying merely on the words of scriptures and instructions that one attains direct realization. It is gained through conviction in the very depths of one's mind, through one's own awareness.

Conviction gained through the path is the path of yoga, the actual knowledge of the meaning of the four kinds of realization. This does not depend on the time it takes for the cause to produce a result. Rather, one gains direct realization and conviction oneself.

It is thanks to three characteristics that culmination in this is attained. An understanding of the four kinds of realization is the characteristic of knowledge. Repeated familiarization is the characteristic of application. Actualization through the power of such familiarization is the characteristic of the result. These three characteristics indicate the connection, the requisite, and the ultimate purpose.

"Connection" refers to the causal characteristic of knowledge. This is the realization that all things that are conceptualized as the phenomena of total affliction and complete purity have, from the very beginning, the nature of the enlightened body, speech, and mind. It is the understanding that all phenomena are, by nature, the ultimate expanse of the enlightened state and that this is the meaning of blessing. This knowledge is the connection with the goal, for it is the cause for accomplishing unsurpassable buddhahood.

"Requisite" refers to the characteristic of application—that is, the enjoyment in the great sameness, without acceptance or rejection, of all things that are conceptualized as the phenomena of total

བདུད་རྩི་ལྔ་ལ་སོགས་པར་བརྟགས་པ་ཐམས་ཅད་ཡེ་ནས་སངས་རྒྱས་པའི་མཉམ་པ་ཆེན་པོ་ལ་བླང་དོར་མེད་པར་སྤྱོད་པ་ནི་འཇུག་པའི་མཚན་ཉིད་དོ། །དེ་ནི་བླ་ན་མེད་པའི་སངས་རྒྱས་སུ་གྲུབ་པའི་རྒྱུ་ཡིན་པའི་ཕྱིར་དགོས་པའོ། །

དགོས་པའི་ཡང་དགོས་པ་ནི། ཀུན་ནས་ཉོན་མོངས་པ་དང་རྣམ་པར་བྱང་བའི་ཆོས་དང་། སྨན་ལྔ་དང་། བདུད་རྩི་ལྔ་སོགས་ཁྱད་པར་དུ་བཏགས་པ་ཐམས་ཅད་ཡེ་ནས་སངས་རྒྱས་པའི་མཉམ་པ་ཆེན་པོའི་ངང་དུ་བླང་དོར་མེད་པར་ལྷུན་གྱིས་གྲུབ་པའི་ཕྱིར། སྲིད་པའི་འཁོར་བ་ཉིད་ཡེ་ནས་བླ་ན་མེད་པར་སངས་རྒྱས་པའི་རང་བཞིན་མྱ་ངན་ལས་འདས་པའི་མཚན་ཉིད་དུ་ལྷུན་གྱིས་གྲུབ་པ་ཡིན་པས་འབྲས་བུའི་མཚན་ཉིད་དེ་སྐུ་གསུང་ཐུགས་མི་ཟད་པ་རྒྱན་གྱི་འཁོར་ལོ་མངོན་སུམ་དུ་གྱུར་པ་ནི་དགོས་པའི་ཡང་དགོས་པའོ། །

དེ་ལ་བསྙེན་པ་དང་། ཉེ་བའི་བསྙེན་པ་དང་། སྒྲུབ་པ་དང་། སྒྲུབ་པ་ཆེན་པོའི་དོན་ལྷུན་གྱིས་གྲུབ་པར་གྱུར་པའི་རྣལ་འབྱོར་ལ་བསྟན་པར་བྱའོ། །

དེ་ལ་བསྙེན་པ་ནི་བྱང་ཆུབ་སེམས་ཤེས་པ་སྟེ། དེ་ཡང་ཆོས་ཐམས་ཅད་ཡེ་ནས་སངས་རྒྱས་པའི་རང་བཞིན་དུ་ལམ་གྱིས་བསྒྲུབ་ཅིང་གཉེན་པོས་བཅོས་སུ་མེད་པར་རྟོགས་པའོ། །

ཉེ་བའི་བསྙེན་པ་ནི་བདག་ཉིད་ལྷར་ཤེས་པ་སྟེ། དེ་ཡང་ཆོས་ཐམས་ཅད་ཡེ་ནས་སངས་རྒྱས་པའི་རང་བཞིན་པས། བདག་ཉིད་ཀྱང་ཡེ་ནས་ལྷའི་རང་བཞིན་ཡིན་གྱི་ད་ལྟ་སྒྲུབ་པ་ནི་མ་ཡིན་པར་རྟོགས་པའོ། །

སྒྲུབ་པ་ནི་ཡུམ་བསྐྱེད་པ་སྟེ། དེ་ཡང་ཡུམ་ཆེན་མོ་ནམ་མཁའི་དབྱིངས་ལས།

affliction and complete purity, the five medicines, the five nectars, and so on, for they are primordially the enlightened state. This is a causal factor for accomplishing unsurpassable enlightenment, and it is therefore requisite.

"Ultimate purpose" refers to the characteristic of the result, for from the very beginning, all things—the phenomena of total affliction and complete purity and, in particular, the five medicines, five nectars, and so forth—are the enlightened state. They are spontaneously present in the state of great sameness, beyond acceptance and rejection. Therefore samsaric existence itself is, from the beginning, spontaneously present as the characteristic of nirvāṇa, the nature of unsurpassable buddhahood. This actualization of the wheel of inexhaustible ornaments—the enlightened body, speech, and mind—is the ultimate purpose.

For this, one must strive in yogic practice, in which the branches of approach, close approach, accomplishment, and great accomplishment are spontaneously present.

"Approach" refers to knowledge of bodhicitta. This is the understanding that phenomena are naturally the enlightened state from the very beginning and are not made so by the path or contrived as such by means of antidotes.

"Close approach" refers to the knowledge that we are ourselves the deity. This is the understanding that since all phenomena are, by nature, the enlightened state from the beginning, we too have been the deity, by nature, from the beginning; it is not something that we are accomplishing only now.

"Accomplishment" refers to the generation of the female deities. This is the understanding that from the expanse of space, the Great

ནམ་མཁའ་ཉིད་ཡུམ་ཆེན་མོ་ས་ཆུ་མེ་རླུང་བཞིར་སྣང་ཞིང་། བྱ་བ་བྱེད་པའི་ཡུམ་ཡེ་ནས་ཡིན་པར་རྟོགས་པའོ། །

སྒྲུབ་པ་ཆེན་པོ་ནི། ཐབས་དང་ཤེས་རབ་འབྲེལ་བ་སྟེ། དེ་ཡང་ཡུམ་ཆེན་མོ་ལྔའི་ཤེས་རབ་དང་ཡུམ་གྱི་མཁའ་སྟོང་པ་ཉིད་ལས། ཕུང་པོ་ལྔ་སངས་རྒྱས་ཐམས་ཅད་ཀྱི་ཡབ་སྐྱོན་པ་མེད་པར་ཡེ་ནས་ཟུང་དུ་གྱུར་པས་འབྲེལ་པ་ལས། བྱང་ཆུབ་སེམས་སྤྲུལ་པ་ལྷུམ་དྲལ་དུ་གྱུར་པའི་རང་བཞིན་ནི། །

ཡེ་ནས་སངས་རྒྱས་པའི་དོན་ལ་སྒྱུ་མ་ལ་སྒྱུ་མ་རོལ་ཅིང་བདེ་མཆོག་སྒྱུ་མའི་རྒྱུན་ལ་བདེ་བའི་དུས་ཉིད་ན། མཚན་མ་མེད་པའི་དོན་མི་དམིགས་མཁའ་དང་སྙོམས་པ་ནི་ཀློང་དུ་གྱུར་ནས་ལྷུན་གྱི་གྲུབ་པ་སྟེ། བདུད་རྣམ་བཞི་ཡང་བརྟུལ་ནས་མཐར་ཕྱིན་པའི་དོན་འགྲུབ་པའོ། །

ཆོས་ཐམས་ཅད་གདོད་མ་ནས་རྣམ་པར་དག་པས། ཡིད་བཞིན་གྱི་གཞལ་ཡས་ཁང་རྒྱ་ཡོངས་སུ་མ་ཆད་པའི་འཁོར་ལོ་ཡེ་ནས་བླ་ན་མེད་པའི་དཀྱིལ་འཁོར་དུ་འཇུག་པ་ཡང་ཐབས་ཀྱི་ཐེག་པའི་གཞུང་ཐོས་པ་ནི་མིག་ཕྱེ་བའོ། །དོན་རྟོགས་པ་ནི་དཀྱིལ་འཁོར་མཐོང་བའོ། །རྟོགས་ནས་གོམས་པར་བྱེད་པ་ནི་དཀྱིལ་འཁོར་དུ་ཞུགས་པའོ། །ཞུགས་ནས་མངོན་དུ་གྱུར་པ་ནི་དངོས་གྲུབ་ཆེན་པོ་ཐོབ་པའོ།།

༄ དེ་ལྟར་ཚུལ་འདི་ནི་རྫོགས་པ་ཆེན་པོའི་མཐར་ཕྱིན་པའི་དོན་ཏོ། ཡི་གེ་འཁོར་ལོ་ཚོགས་ཆེན་གྱི་ས་ལ་ལྷུན་གྱིས་འཇུག་པ་སྟེ། སྐྱེས་བུ་བློ་རྩལ་རབ་ཀྱིས་ཡེ་ནས་སངས་རྒྱས་པའི་དོན་ལ་ཡེ་ནས་སངས་རྒྱས་པར་རིག་ནས། གོམ་པ་དྲུག་དལ་དུ་འགྲོ་བ་ཡིན་གྱི་ཕལ་གྱི་བྱ་བ་ནི་མ་ཡིན་ནོ། །

Mother, space itself appears in the form of the four great mothers—earth, water, fire, and wind—and that they are, from the beginning, the mothers that perform all activities.

"Great accomplishment" refers to the interconnection of skillful means and wisdom. From the primordial union of the wisdoms of the five great mothers and the five aggregates (the fathers of all the buddhas appearing without expectancy from the emptiness-space of the mother), bodhicitta manifests in the form of the male and female bodhisattvas.

Within the state of primordial enlightenment, illusion delights in illusion, and at the moment of bliss in the illusory stream of supreme bliss, the absence of all characteristics equal to space beyond all reference is fully realized and is spontaneously present. The four demons are subdued and the ultimate goal is achieved.

All phenomena are perfectly pure from the beginning and are a maṇḍala beyond all dimension, a vast and measureless palace that grants every wish. To enter this primordial, unsurpassable maṇḍala, one must open one's eyes, which is achieved by hearing the texts of the vehicles of skillful means. To understand their meaning is to behold the maṇḍala. To gain familiarity, once one has understood, is to enter the maṇḍala. And when, once entered, the maṇḍala becomes manifest, the great accomplishment is attained.

This method is the culmination, the Great Perfection. The level of the Great Wheel of Collections of Syllables is spontaneously entered. Beings with the sharpest faculties have understood that primordial enlightenment means that they have been enlightened from the very beginning, and they progress powerfully on the path. Their actions are not the actions of ordinary beings.

ཕལ་གྱིས་ཐོས་ཏེ་ཇི་ལྟར་བསམ་ཀྱང་བདེན་ཞིང་ཟབ་པར་ཡིད་ཆེས་པར་མི་འགྱུར་རོ། །ཡིད་ཆེས་པ་དང་ཕལ་གྱི་བློ་ལ་གོ་དཀའ་ཞིང་བདེན་པ་དང་ཟབ་པར་མ་ཤེས་པས་ཉམས་དང་སྨྲར་ནས། ཀུན་ཀྱང་དེ་དང་འདྲ་སླམ་ནས་ཡོངས་བརྫུན་ཞེས་སྐྱེས་བུ་རབ་ལ་སྐུར་པ་འདེབས་ཤིང་སུན་འབྱིན་པའི་བློ་སྐྱེ་བར་འགྱུར་བས་རབ་ཏུ་གསང་བའི་ཕྱིར་ཡང་གསང་བའི་ཐེག་པ་ཞེས་བཀའ་སྩལ་ཏེ། །

དེ་བས་ན་ཆོས་ཐམས་ཅད་ཡེ་ནས་སངས་རྒྱས་པའི་དོན་ལ་རྟོགས་པའི་བློ་མ་སྐྱེས་བར་དུ་ཐེག་པ་འོག་མ་པས་འགྲོ་བའི་དོན་བྱས་ན་གདུལ་བྱ་ཆུད་མི་ཟ་བར་སློབ་དཔོན་གྱིས་འཁོར་བའི་སྐྱོན་དང་། མྱ་ངན་ལས་འདས་པའི་ཡོན་ཏན་དང་། ཐེག་པ་མཐའ་དག་ལ་མཁས་པར་བྱ་བ་ཡིན་གྱི། ཕྱོགས་འགའ་མི་ཤེས་པས་སློབ་དཔོན་གྱིས་བཟུང་དུ་མི་རུང་བར་རྒྱ་ཆེར་འབྱུང་ངོ།།

༄ ལྟ་བའི་ཁྱད་པར་གྱི་དཀའ་ཐུབ་དང་བརྟུལ་ཞུགས་ཀྱང་བྱེ་བྲག་ཏུ་འགྱུར་ཏེ། དཀའ་ཐུབ་མེད་པ་ནི། འཇིག་རྟེན་ཕྱལ་བ་དང་མུར་ཐུག་གོ །དཀའ་ཐུབ་ཡོད་པ་ནི་རྣམ་པ་བཞི་སྟེ་རྒྱང་འཕེན་དང་། མུ་སྟེགས་པ་སྟེ། འཇིག་རྟེན་གྱི་བཀའ་ཐུབ་དང་། ཉན་ཐོས་ཀྱི་དཀའ་ཐུབ་དང་། བྱང་ཆུབ་སེམས་དཔའི་དཀའ་ཐུབ་དང་། བླ་ན་མེད་པའི་བཀའ་ཐུབ་པོ། །

དེ་ལ་ཕྱལ་བ་ནི་རྒྱུ་འབྲས་ལ་རྨོངས་པའི་ཕྱིར་བཀའ་ཐུབ་མེད་པའོ། །མུར་ཐུག་པ་ནི་ཆད་པར་ལྟ་བའི་ཕྱིར་བཀའ་ཐུབ་མེད་པའོ། །རྒྱང་འཕེན་པ་ནི་ཚེ་འདིའི་ཁྱད་པར་སྒྲུབ་པའི་ཕྱིར་གཙང་སྦྲ་ལ་སོགས་པའི་དཀའ་ཐུབ་ཅན་ནོ། །མུ་སྟེགས་ན་བདག་རྟག་པ་ཞིག་ཡོད་པ་དེ་དག་པར་བྱ་བའི་ཕྱིར། ལུས་སུན་འབྱིན་ཅིང་མེ་ལྔ་བརྟེན་པ་ལ་སོགས་པའི་བཀའ་ཐུབ་དང་།

However much ordinary people may hear and reflect on this, they will not gain confidence in its truth and profundity. Since it is difficult to have confidence and to understand it with their ordinary minds and they do not recognize how true and profound it is, they judge by their own experience and think it is the same for everyone. "It's all a pack of lies," they say, belittling superior beings and giving rise to an attitude of repudiation. This is why this teaching is extremely secret and also why it is called the Secret Vehicle.

Therefore, until their disciples have understood that all phenomena are primordially the enlightened state, teachers use the lower vehicles to benefit beings; and to avoid wasting those beings' potential, they should be well versed in the defects of saṃsāra, the qualities of nirvāṇa, and all the vehicles. Disciples should not be guided by a teacher who is ignorant of some aspects. All this has been extensively taught.

Along with the different views, there are also specific kinds of spiritual training and yogic discipline. Those who have no spiritual training are the unreflective and the nihilistic extremists. Those who have a spiritual training display four kinds of practices: the mundane trainings of the materialists and eternalistic extremists, the spiritual training of the listeners, the spiritual training of the bodhisattvas, and the unsurpassable spiritual training.

The unreflective are ignorant with regard to the karmic law of cause and effect, and they do not, therefore, engage in spiritual training. Neither do the nihilistic extremists, for they have nihilistic views. The materialists, in order to achieve advantage in this life, engage in practices such as ritual cleanliness. The eternalistic extremists, in order to purify the self that they believe exists, indulge

བརྟུལ་ཞུགས་ལོག་པར་སྤྱོད་པའོ། །

ཉན་ཐོས་ཀྱི་དཀའ་ཐུབ་ནི། འདུལ་བ་ལས། །

སྡིག་པ་ཅི་ཡང་མི་བྱ་སྟེ།

དགེ་བ་ཕུན་སུམ་ཚོགས་པར་སྤྱོད། །

རང་གི་སེམས་ནི་ཡོངས་སུ་འདུལ།

འདི་ནི་སངས་རྒྱས་བསྟན་པ་ཡིན། ཞེས་འབྱུང་སྟེ། །

དགེ་བ་དང་མི་དགེ་བའི་ཆོས་ཐམས་ཅད་ཀུན་རྫོབ་དང་དོན་དམ་པར་གཉིས་ཀ་སོ་སོར་ཡོད་པར་ལྟ་བ་དང་། དགེ་བ་ནི་སྤྱོད་མི་དགེ་བ་ནི་སྤང་བའི་དཀའ་ཐུབ་དང་བརྟུལ་ཞུགས་སྤྱོད་པའོ། །

བྱང་ཆུབ་སེམས་དཔའི་དཀའ་ཐུབ་ནི། །བྱང་ཆུབ་སེམས་དཔའི་སྡོམ་པ་ལས། །

རྐྱེན་དུ་འཚམ་པར་དོན་མི་བྱེད། །

རྫུ་འཕྲུལ་བསྒྲིགས་ལ་སོགས་མི་བྱེད། །

སྙིང་རྗེར་ལྡན་ཞིང་བྱམས་ཕྱིར་དང་། །

སེམས་དགེ་བ་ལ་ཉེས་པ་མེད། ཅེས་འབྱུང་སྟེ། །

སྙིང་རྗེ་ཆེན་པོས་ཟིན་ན་ཆོས་ཐམས་ཅད་དགེ་བ་དང་མི་དགེ་བ་གང་སྤྱད་ཀྱང་སྡོམ་པ་ཉམས་པར་མི་འགྱུར་ཏེ། བྱང་ཆུབ་སེམས་དཔའི་སྡོམ་པ་ནི། མདོར་ན་སྙིང་རྗེ་ཆེན་པོས་གཞི་བཟུང་ནས་སྤྱོད་དོ། །

བླ་ན་མེད་པའི་དཀའ་ཐུབ་ནི། དམ་ཚིག་ཆེན་པོའི་མདོ་ལས། །

mistakenly in austerities, such as the mortification of the body and the ordeal of five fires, and in yogic disciplines.

The disciplines of the listeners are described in the Vinaya:

> Abandon every evil deed,
> Practice virtue well
> And perfectly subdue your mind:
> This is Buddha's teaching.

The listeners consider that positive and negative phenomena exist on both the relative and ultimate levels, and they follow the spiritual training and yogic discipline of implementing virtue and avoiding negativity.

The spiritual training of the bodhisattvas is described in *The Vows of a Bodhisattva*:

> Failure to benefit as circumstances dictate,
> Failure to use miraculous powers to intimidate and so on—
> Such faults are absent in those whose intentions are
> virtuous,
> For they are filled with compassion and love.

Whatever bodhisattvas do, positive or negative, if they are imbued with great compassion, they will not damage their vows. For, the bodhisattva vow, in brief, is to act on the basis of great compassion.

The unsurpassable training is described in the *Sūtra of the Great Samaya*:

སངས་རྒྱས་ཐེག་པ་རབ་ངེས་ནི། །

ཉོན་མོངས་འདོད་ལྷ་ཀུན་སྤྱོད་ཀྱང་། །

པདྨ་ལ་ནི་འདམ་བཞིན་ཏེ། །

དེ་ལ་ཚུལ་ཁྲིམས་ཕུན་སུམ་ཚོགས། ཞེས་འབྱུང་སྟེ། །

ཆོས་ཐམས་ཅད་ཡེ་ནས་མཉམ་པ་ཉིད་ཀྱི་ཕྱིར། སྙིང་རྗེ་ནི་བསྙེན་དུ་མེད་ལ། ཞེ་སྡང་ནི་སྤང་དུ་མེད་དེ། དེ་ལྟར་མ་རྟོགས་པ་ལ་ཐུགས་རྗེ་མི་འབྱུང་བར་མ་ཡིན་ཏེ། །

ཇི་ལྟར་ལྟ་བས་ཡེ་ནས་རྣམ་པར་དག་པར་རྟོགས་པ་བཞིན་དུ་དཀའ་ཐུབ་དང་བརྟུལ་ཞུགས་ཀྱང་དེ་ལྟར་རྣམ་པར་དག་པར་སྤྱོད་དོ། །

ལྟ་བའི་ཕྲེང་བ་གསང་བ་འདི། །

དངུལ་ཡོང་རང་ཕྱེ་མིག་རྐེད་ལྟར། །

ཤེས་རབ་ཐབས་ཀྱི་རྩལ་འཆང་བའི། །

སྐྱེས་མཆོག་ཡོད་ན་འཕྲད་གྱུར་ཅིག །

ལྟ་བའི་ཕྲེང་བ་ཞེས་བྱ་བའི་མན་ངག་རྫོགས་སོ།། །།

In those who have the utmost certainty with regard to
Buddha's vehicle,
Even indulgence in all five defilements and sense pleasures
Will be the very height of discipline,
As unstained as lotus petals unsullied by the mud.

All phenomena are in the state of sameness from the beginning, so compassion is not something to be cultivated and anger is not something to be eschewed. This does not mean, however, that compassion does not arise for those who fail to understand.

And to the extent that, as far as one's view is concerned, one has realized primordial perfect purity, one's spiritual training and yogic discipline will also be perfectly pure.

Like those born blind who spontaneously gain their sight,
If there are superior beings
Who hold the power of wisdom and skillful means,
May they encounter this secret Garland of Views.

This completes the pith instruction entitled *A Garland of Views*.

A Treasury of Gems

A Commentary by Annotation of the
Great Master Padmasambhava's Pith Instruction
A Garland of Views

Jamgön Mipham

Jamgön Mipham

Jamgön Mipham

The illustration of Jamgön Mipham that appears on p. 30 of *A Garland of Views* was inadvertently transposed. This sticker contains the corrected illustration and can be placed over the transposed image.

Namo Guru Padma Mañjuśrī ye

Glorious Buddha, Lotus-Born,
You who hold the treasure of omniscient wisdom,
Exponent of the various different vehicles,
Orgyen, knower of the three times, care for me.

Here is an explanation of the pith instruction *A Garland of Views*, a treatise indisputably ascribed to the great master Padmasambhava. It comprises three sections: an introduction, the main body of the text, and a conclusion. The first of these is divided into an explanation of the title and an expression of veneration.

I. Introduction

A. Explanation of the title

> **A memory aid summarizing the distinctive features of the views and vehicles.**

In the *Guhyagarbha-tantra*, which is the glory of all the tantras and explanatory teachings that show how all phenomena are, from the very beginning, spontaneously present as the Great Perfection, we read:

No understanding, wrong understanding,
Partial understanding, nonunderstanding of the ultimately
true nature,
Discipline, mind, secret, and natural secret.
The meanings of these are present in the vajra mind of the
teacher
Who perfectly demonstrates them by means of phrases
That depend on the assemblage of names designated by
language,
Drawing out the meaning hidden within.

Consistent with the intellects of different kinds of individuals, there are various mundane and supramundane philosophical views:

- two for those who have no understanding (the ordinary unreflective and the materialists)
- two for those who understand wrongly (non-Buddhist extremists, who are either nihilistic or eternalistic)
- two for those who only partly understand (listeners and solitary realizers)
- the view of those who have not realized the ultimately true nature—namely, bodhisattvas who follow the way of the transcendent perfections
- the view associated with the discipline of Kriyātantra
- the view associated with the wisdom mind in Yogatantra
- two views associated with the secret methods of the generation and perfection phases in the inner Mantra Vehicle of the Great Yoga[1]

- the view associated with the method of the natural secret Great Perfection

In particular, there are the three vehicles of characteristics (listener, solitary realizer, and bodhisattva), the three outer mantra vehicles (Kriyā, Upa, and Yoga), and the three inner mantra vehicles (generation, perfection, and Great Perfection), together making nine successive vehicles that are paths to perfect liberation. In order to ensure that the king and twenty-five disciples and others with fortunate karma would not forget these distinctions, the Guru himself composed this short text as a memory aid, briefly describing all the particular features of these views and their respective results, and giving it a title that befits its contents.

B. Expression of veneration

I pay homage to the Lord Mañjuśrī the youthful, and to Vajradharma.

Homage is paid to the deity of wisdom according to the causal vehicle of characteristics—namely, to him who has destroyed the two kinds of obscurations together with their habitual tendencies, who possesses the six qualities of excellence (qualities of the transcendent perfections both as cause and result),[2] and who has therefore gone beyond the extremes of existence and peace. He takes the form of the youthful bodhisattva Mañjuśrī ("Gentle and Glorious"), who is gentle because his mind, the ultimate nature, is unafflicted by mental elaboration, and who is glorious because he has achieved the twofold goal.

Homage is also paid, in accordance with the resultant vehicle of secret mantra, to the yidam deity, the Lord of Secrets, Vajradharma ("Adamantine Dharma"). His name refers to the indestructible or adamantine nature of things (namely, their emptiness unaffected by attributes or concepts) and to his manifesting as unobstructed compassion or as the personification of the Dharma, the Buddha's teachings.

II. The main body of the text

The actual text is divided into explanations of (A) the different views and (B) the different kinds of yogic disciplines. The first of these explanations is divided into non-Buddhist and Buddhist views, each of which consists of a brief outline and a detailed explanation.

A. Explanation of the different views

1. Explanation of non-Buddhists' views

a. Brief introduction

> **The false views entertained by beings in the world are without number, but they can be summarized as being of four kinds: those of the unreflective, the materialists, the nihilistic extremists and the eternalistic extremists.**

The outer universe—the sphere of disintegration, the world composed of perishable things—is inhabited by sentient beings who are imputed merely on that which the mind fails to discern as the continua of the five aggregates. These people are immersed in ignorance. They stray from the truth, and through their mistaken understanding and various distorted beliefs, they exhibit innumerable views; for there is no limit to false understanding. Nevertheless, these views can be summarized as being of four kinds. (The Tibetan word for "kind"—*rnam pa*—has several different meanings: cause, particularity, similarity, appearance, number, and condition. Here it should be understood in the numerical sense.)

These four are the views of

- the unreflective, who have no philosophy of life or spiritual practice, and are destitute of any kind of deeper purpose
- the materialists, whose name in Tibetan (pronounced "gyang penpa") has different meanings depending on how it is spelled—either *rgyang phen pa* (literally, "rejectionists"), because in their thoughts and behavior, materialists lay aside any concern for future existences, rejecting them as far away; or *rgyang phan pa* (literally, "seekers of obvious benefit"), because they act only for what is obviously beneficial for this present life and have no greater aim
- the nihilistic extremists (Skt. *naiṣṭhika*)[3]
- the eternalistic extremists (Skt. *tīrthika*), called *mu stegs pa* in Tibetan because they are said to stay on the steps (*stegs*) leading down to the edge (*mu*) of the river, that is—the path flowing into the ocean of nirvāṇa[4]

The term "materialist," when it is not being used specifically, may denote any non-Buddhist outside the Dharma, as is the case in the *Parinirvāṇa Sūtra*, where there is a debate between Lord Buddha's point of view and that of the "materialists." But here in the context of a description of the four kinds of views, the general word has a specific usage and is employed in a particular way for the view mentioned in this text. Moreover, the term does not refer here to those with wrong understanding, the "materialists" (*lokāyatika*) who are the followers of Bṛhaspati and hold nihilistic views, like the nihilistic extremists. It refers, rather, to those without any understanding. These materialists and the unreflective resemble each other in that they fail to investigate the karmic law of cause and effect, but they differ in that the former do display some slight sagacity in securing the purposes of this life, while the others are marked by a particular lack of clarity. The latter comprise most of the beings in the higher realms. Consequently, the expression "those who do what is beneficial for this present life" has to be understood in context: if it is invariably taken to refer to the followers of Bṛhaspati and the like, the meaning intended in the root text will be misunderstood. An understanding of the context of words with a wide range of meanings[5] is indispensable for explaining all the treatises.

Similarly also, where the *naiṣṭhika* (literally, "extremist," Tib. *mur thug pa*) are mentioned in the *Kāśyapa Chapter*—"Kāśyapa, my teaching cannot be destroyed by the ninety-six extremists: it will be destroyed by my monks who are similar to me"—the Buddha was speaking of non-Buddhists in general. And the term *tīrthika* (Tib. *mu stegs pa*) is also used generally for the non-Buddhist proponents of eternalism and nihilism. In this text, however, the two terms *naiṣṭhika* and *tīrthika* should be taken as general names for the proponents of nihilism and eternalism, respectively. Only then will the terms properly correspond with what they mean and reflect the intended meaning of this text.[6]

Now with regard to all these, an analogy can be made with a precious jewel placed at a crossroads. Some people will not see it at all, some will see it as a semiprecious stone, some will see it as any common precious thing, and others will see it as it is. Those who do not see it at all ("not seeing" here being categorized with the others as a way of seeing) are analogous to the materialists and the unreflective, who are presented together in that they do not understand the true and ultimate status of phenomena. Like the kinds of beings who are mostly found in the lower realms, they are as dull and stupid as cattle, not even knowing how to think in terms of earlier and later existences. Theirs is the lowest of views, for it is impossible to get any lower. It could be argued that since they do not follow a path, it is inappropriate to say that they have a view. However, because their minds are saturated with ignorance, their "view" is in fact a state of not having any understanding. Consequently, when one is establishing the proper view, their position is something to be rejected. In this respect, while most beings cling to substantial existence and abide by the view of the transitory composite,[7] on account of their feeble thinking and understanding, they consider cause and result to be real and are oppressed by the gloom of their view in which nothing is specifically analyzed. This is why we speak of their having a view.

b. Detailed explanation

i. Explanation of the unreflective and the materialists

> **The unreflective have no understanding as to whether or not phenomena are the causes or results of anything. They are completely confused.**

What do we mean by the unreflective? They are those who have no understanding at all of the existence or otherwise of the karmic causes that produce all the phenomena we perceive externally and internally and the results that they produce. They are completely unthinking, utterly ignorant and bewildered with regard to the karmic law of cause of effect.

> **The materialists have no understanding as to whether or not there are previous and future lives. They work to achieve strength, riches, and power in this one life, for which they rely on the secret knowledge of worldly beings.**

The materialists—rejectionists or seekers of obvious benefit—have no understanding of whether or not there are previous and future lives and put their efforts into the various methods for achieving strength, riches, and power in this one life. For this, they rely on the explanations of worldly teachers (which do not lead to perfect liberation) in order to achieve goals limited to their present existence: securing a livelihood, the practice of astrology, the study of politics, and so on. They also have recourse to the secret knowledge of the world, the black magic of Benares, divination rituals, the subjugation of demons, the propitiation of local deities, and the performance of wealth rituals, whether in person or through the agency of others.

ii. Explanation of the nihilistic extremists and eternalistic extremists

> **Nihilistic extremists do not believe that things have causes and effects. For them, everything that comes about in this one life does so "just like that" and finally is extinguished.**
>
> **Eternalistic extremists believe in a permanent self, which they imagine to be present in all phenomena. Some believe in a reality—an effect—for which there is no cause. Some have an incorrect view of causality. Some believe that whereas the cause is real, the effects are unreal.**

The nihilistic extremists have a nihilistic view. They think that all phenomena that fall within their purview are devoid of any kind of karmic law of cause and effect. All the phenomena that arise in their one and only life, rather than being propelled by the deeds of previous lives, have come into being just like that, like mushrooms in a field or bubbles on water, and in the end they are extinguished like lamps.

The eternalistic extremists believe that the unreal self that they impute to phenomena (things that exist within a causal sequence) exists permanently. Among the eternalistic extremists, there are those who believe that the cause of everything is "nature" or prakṛti. Prakṛti is not produced from causes and conditions, and within its nature, all phenomena evolve. For this reason, they say that prakṛti and its aspects (phenomena) are not different from each other. Consequently, puruṣa, the self, is said to be isolated and whole within itself. Their view, moreover, is that phenomena exist within prakṛti like this from the beginning and there is no other cause that produces them. It is thus that these extremists "believe in a reality—an effect—for which there is no cause." One might well ask how they can say that there is an effect that does not depend on a cause. To which they would reply that existence is indeed an effect—in the sense that it is accomplished—in the same way that one says that space is accomplished primordially. This is their single principle.[8]

Those who "have an incorrect view of causality" believe in the person of an Almighty God,[9] who exists from all eternity. This permanent entity has created all things, animate and inanimate, and has power over them. And in order to propitiate this all-powerful being, they sacrifice large numbers of animals and so on. Their view comprises two beliefs: a permanent God and impermanent manifestations. Their assertions amount to saying that nonvirtuous actions can lead to higher rebirth, or that a permanent cause can give rise to impermanent results.[10]

Those who consider that "whereas the cause is real, the effects are unreal" believe in a creator as a causal factor. They assert a permanent self the size of a thumb and so on, like a little bird that flies out when the pot containing it is broken. They have three beliefs: they claim that the permanent self only performs the function of a cause; they claim that the nature of its resulting creations, the aggregates, is phenomena that are impermanent and changing; and they claim that the results themselves only occur once—they do not have the potential to create other aggregates and the process stops there.[11]

These extreme positions of eternalism and nihilism include all aspects, without exception, of non-Buddhist eternalistic and nihilistic beliefs.

All these are the views of ignorance.

The four views described above are all analogous to ignorance, the opposite of knowledge. In this section, which describes the positions of worldly beings, Padmasambhava confined himself to a description of their views. He did not discuss their paths and results, for he considered that this would serve no purpose.

2. Explanation of Buddhists' views

a. Brief introduction

The path that leads beyond the world has two aspects: the vehicle of characteristics and the Diamond Vehicle.

The supramundane path leading beyond the world, which is related to the untainted path, can be divided into two vehicles. The vehicle of characteristics teaches the general and specific characteristics of phenomena and the characteristics of total affliction and complete purity separately and distinctly, showing what is to be abandoned and what is to be adopted. The Diamond Vehicle teaches that total affliction and complete purity are essentially inseparable and unchanging as the maṇḍala of the enlightened body, speech, and mind.

b. Detailed explanation

i. Presentation of the vehicle of characteristics

A) Brief introduction

The vehicle of characteristics has three further divisions: the Listener Vehicle, the Solitary Realizer Vehicle, and the Bodhisattva Vehicle.

For the vehicle of characteristics, there are three further divisions, based on the degree of clinging to those characteristics by beings with different fortunes, aspirations, and faculties. These are

- the vehicle of the listeners, who themselves listen to the instructions given by others and then cause others to listen to them
- the vehicle of the solitary realizers, who realize their result, the truth, all by themselves during their final existence
- the vehicle of the bodhisattvas, heroes of enlightenment or enlightenment beings, so named either because of their steadfast intention to attain enlightenment or because of their focusing on enlightenment and sentient beings[12]

B) Detailed explanation

1) Explanation of the Listener Vehicle

The followers of the Listener Vehicle believe that the views of the eternalistic extremists and so on amount to conceptual exaggerations and depreciations of phenomena as a whole. They thus consider that the nihilistic view that things have

never existed and the eternalist view that they exist permanently and so on are as invalid as the belief that a rope is a snake. They consider that the infinitesimal particles of the four great elements that make up the aggregates, elements, senses-and-fields, and so forth, and also the instants of consciousness, exist on the ultimate level. By meditating on the Four Noble Truths, they progressively accomplish the four results.

The view of those individuals who have engaged in the Listener Vehicle—that is, the appropriate path that enables them to attain the listeners' goal—comprises the philosophical tenets that have been established with wisdom and in which they accordingly have definite faith. This is taught here in terms of three aspects: view, meditation, and result.

In terms of philosophical view, the views of the non-Buddhist eternalistic extremists and others are conceptual imputations concerning the whole of phenomena—that is, the aggregates, elements, and senses-and-fields. These imputations take the form of exaggeration and depreciation. On the one hand, non-Buddhists take as permanent what is not so, and on the other hand, they consider as nonexistent what in fact exists. Their views comprise the view of nihilism (that things have never existed or do not exist at all) and the view of eternalism (that they have permanent existence and so on). The listeners consider these views to be no more valid than the imaginary snake one might think is present when one sees a rope in poor light. Their view of the nature of the aggregates, elements, and senses-and-fields, which, just like the rope in the example, are the basis of appearance,[13] is as follows. For them, the tiniest particles of the four great elements, which give rise to gross appearances (the outer material world of forms and suchlike), and the instants of consciousness (the inner mind) exist ultimately or truly. There are two schools of thought here—the Vaibhāṣika and the Sautrāntika—between which there is some slight disagreement. For example, the former holds that uncompounded phenomena are permanent, while the latter asserts that like the son of a barren woman, they are completely nonexistent. And among the Vaibhāṣikas, there are numerous subtle disagreements on individual points of view. Nevertheless, they are all similar in asserting that ultimately particles and instants exist truly. They are therefore presented together.

Their meditation consists of the stages of concentration along with meditation on the Four Noble Truths—suffering, origin, cessation, and path. These are "truths" because they are without error concerning the nature of things as they are, and they are "noble" because they are realized by sublime beings, or alternatively, because they are noble by nature.[14] With regard to these truths, listeners focus on the four truths related to the three worlds and meditate on them in the form of their sixteen subdivisions.

In due course, there arises the gnosis of the path of seeing, which comprises the sixteen instants of knowing and acceptance. Subsequently, they progressively eliminate the defilements related to the nine levels of the three worlds that have to be eliminated one by one on the path of meditation. In this way, they achieve four results. When they are freed from the first three or four of the nine degrees of defilement of the world of desire, they attain the level of stream-enterer. When they have eliminated the sixth degree of defilement, they attain the level of once-returner.[15] When the ninth has been eliminated, they attain the level of nonreturner. And when all the defilements of the peak of existence have been eliminated, they attain the level of arhat.

2) Explanation of the Solitary Realizer Vehicle

Those engaged in the Solitary Realizer Vehicle agree with the listeners in denying the permanent self and so forth imagined by the eternalistic extremists and others, with their conceptual exaggerations and depreciations of the whole of phenomena. But they differ from them in that they have partially realized the absence of self in phenomena related to the aggregate of form. And unlike the listeners, when they attain the result (enlightenment as solitary realizers), they do so without relying on a spiritual teacher. It is, rather, by the force of previous habituation that they realize the profound ultimate nature of phenomena in terms of the twelve links of dependent arising and subsequently attain the result: the solitary realizers' enlightenment.

The view of those who have engaged in the Solitary Realizer Vehicle—that is, the path enabling them to attain the nature of the uncompounded essence that is the solitary realizers' result—is similar to that of the listeners. It negates the permanent self, the nihilistic reality, and so forth, ascribed by the extremists to the whole of phenomena, whether by exaggeration or depreciation. The solitary realizers differ from the listeners in that they have realized the absence of the phenomenal self with regard to the aggregate of form (one of the five aggregates) or, more precisely, the aggregate of form comprising the ten senses-and-fields with form, the ten constituents with form, and the imperceptible forms that make up one part of the constituent "mental objects."[16] By training in this, they eventually, in their final existence, attain their result—enlightenment as solitary realizers. Unlike the listeners, they do not rely at that time on a spiritual teacher.

How they meditate is as follows. As a result of their previous habituation, acquired through following a buddha and training on the level of Beholding Virtue[17] and others, they realize the meaning of the twelve links of dependent arising, whose nature is the four truths. The seven links related to suffering correspond to the truth of suffering. The three related to defilements and the two related to karmic action correspond to the origin.[18] Divestment of those factors of total affliction[19] corresponds to the truth of cessation. And the path that leads to this, involving the realization of, and subsequent habituation to, the meaning of interdependence, corresponds to the truth of the path.

According to another approach, each of the twelve links has four aspects. The attainment of each link corresponds to the truth of suffering, the fact that each link is the condition for the production of the next corresponds to the origin, the halting of each link by the halting of the link preceding it corresponds to the truth of cessation, and correct meditation on the nature of each link in order to bring it to a halt is the path. Thus, for each of the links there arise the sixteen instants of gnosis that take the four truths as their object, so that there are 192 instants of gnosis. These arise at a single sitting, and subsequently the result, enlightenment as a solitary realizer, is attained. By such means, these beings realize the illusion-like ultimate nature of phenomena, the profound meaning. Although they remain in an inexpressible concentration where speech is completely halted, they still entertain the notion "It is inexpressible," because they have not eliminated the concept of an apprehending subject.

Dependent arising is a path common to all Buddhist vehicles. In the case of the listeners, their strong adherence to the characteristics of cause and result dispels the non-Buddhists' wrong understanding of causation. The solitary realizers understand dependent arising on a deeper level, realizing that there is no intrinsic essence related to cause and result existing as an apprehended object. The Yogācārins have even deeper realization, understanding that there are no substantial causes or results existing as an apprehending self. And the Mādhyamikas realize that no substantial cause or result exists even as the nature of reflexive consciousness, thereby completely pacifying all elaborations.

Following the practice of the path just described, there comes the result, which is the solitary realizers' enlightenment, attained either by practice in groups or, rhinoceros-like, in solitude.

3) Explanation of the Bodhisattva Vehicle

The view of those engaged in the Bodhisattva Vehicle is that, on the ultimate level, all phenomena, whether of total affliction or of complete purity, are devoid of inherent existence, while on the relative level, they are mere illusions, each with its

own distinct characteristics. As a result of their training in the ten transcendent perfections, bodhisattvas proceed in stages through the ten levels, at the end of which, they attain unsurpassable enlightenment.

The Bodhisattva Vehicle takes its name from its cause. Its result is no different from that of the secret mantras, so both the Mantra Vehicle and the vehicle of the transcendent perfections constitute the same Great Vehicle. However, they differ in their path, which here is the vehicle of characteristics.[20] The view of those engaged in this vehicle is that the whole of the total affliction that is saṃsāra, in both cause and result, and of the complete purity that is nirvāṇa, in both cause and result, is completely devoid of inherent or true existence on the ultimate level. The essence of the ultimate truth is freedom from mental elaboration, and it is called ultimate because it is the object of the ultimate gnosis, or because it is the highest of all attainments. The ultimate truth can be divided into two kinds: the nominal ultimate truth, in which conceptual elaborations have been partially annulled, and the ultimate truth in itself, where all conceptual elaborations have been completely pacified.

The relative (literally, "all-covering") truth is deluded consciousness together with appearances. It is so called because the true condition of things is "covered"—that is, veiled and conceptualized, by obscurations or by adventitious deluded thoughts. It is subdivided into correct relative truth and mistaken relative truth.[21] As far as this relative truth is concerned, phenomena, which lack true existence, appear in the manner of mere illusions. Here the word "mere" excludes them from being established as real. On the level of mere appearance,[22] things have the ability to fulfill their respective functions and it would be wrong to deny them, saying that they do not exist. They are objects of pure and impure experience and have individual, distinct characteristics, for they exist on the level of conventional evaluative methods of valid cognition.

Provisionally, things are thus ascertained in terms of the two kinds of valid cognition, and on the ultimate level, they are correctly established as the great sameness free of elaboration, the union of appearance and emptiness, the inseparability of the two truths. Once this has been done, there follows the path of meditation. This is indicated by "the ten transcendent perfections," referring to the ten virtuous practices (generosity and the rest) imbued with wisdom—and of all the various kinds of wisdom, the supreme and most perfect is nondual gnosis. The expression "transcendent perfections" is used for these ten virtuous practices because they "go beyond," in the sense that they attain to what we call the ultimate reality free of elaboration, which is not an object of the intellect but transcends it, and also because they go to the other side of the ocean of saṃsāra. There are thus two ways to apply this expression on the path.

Practicing in this way, bodhisattvas proceed in stages through the ten levels, which are the intermediate results of the practice. Its final result is the accomplishment of unsurpassable enlightenment, characterized by the completion of all the host of qualities, such as those of strength and fearlessness,[23] which are superior to those of the listeners and solitary realizers.

ii. Presentation of the Mantra Vehicle

A) Brief introduction

The Diamond Vehicle is also divided into three: the vehicle of Kriyātantra, the vehicle of Ubhayatantra, and the vehicle of Yogatantra.

The Diamond Vehicle is also divided into three, as follows:

- Kriyātantra, in which it is held that, although inner concentration is certainly the principal cause, accomplishment is not attained without depending on outer activities such as cleanliness and ascetic practices
- Ubhayatantra, which holds that accomplishment is attained by means of both outer activities and inner concentration
- Yogatantra, which holds that even without depending on outer activities, accomplishment is attained by concentration alone

B) Detailed explanation

1) Presentation of Kriyātantra

The view of those engaged in the vehicle of Kriyātantra is that, on the ultimate level, there is no arising or cessation. On this basis, they meditate, on the relative level, on the form body of the deity. By the power of bringing together the image of the deity's body, the implements symbolizing the deity's mind, the recitation of the mantra, and the requisite elements (above all, the observance of cleanliness, particular moments in time, the

planets, constellations, and so forth), along with the cause and conditions, accomplishment is gained.

The view of those who have engaged in the vehicle of Kriyātantra is as follows. On the ultimate level, they meditate on the fact that all phenomena are devoid of any intrinsic nature that arises and ceases, while on the relative level, they meditate on the form body of a deity. Those who meditate in this way and who possess the bodhicitta as well as the three principles are explained as being suitable vessels for accomplishment. The three principles are the principle of one's own nature, the principle of the deity, and the principle of recitation. These three include, respectively, the nature of the phenomena of saṃsāra, the attributes of nirvāṇa, and the attributes of the means for accomplishing the latter.

The principle of one's own nature concerns the "self," which is simply the five aggregates taken as a single object unexamined by the intellect. The nature of that self, according to the listeners, is empty in being devoid of conceptual structures such as self and "mine-ness," eternalism and nihilism, as propounded by the extremists. The listeners do not, however, go as far as saying that phenomena like the aggregates do not exist at all.[24] For the Yogācārins, it is empty in being devoid of the conceptual structures of the listeners' concepts of subject and object, but they do not go as far as saying that reflexive awareness—the mind and mental events—does not exist at all. And for the Mādhyamikas, it is empty in being devoid of the Cittamātrins' concepts of the nonconceptual wisdom existing ultimately; for them, the nature of the self is a state of complete pacification of all conceptual attributes.[25]

The principle of the deity comprises six elements of the secret mantra: emptiness, sound, and so on, which are known as the "six deities."[26] The principle of one's own nature is like a golden plate, covered with, as it were, the principle of the deity, which is like refined quicksilver. On this, it is held, one repeatedly meditates.

The principle of recitation has three essential states, three great images, three objects of concentration, and four branches.

The three essential states are gnosis, name, and form. Having realized that, on the ultimate level, the pure nature of the deity and one's own impure nature are not two separate entities, one meditates accordingly. One thus comes to know that pure self-cognizing awareness, which is the gnosis of the deity, and impure awareness, which is the knowledge of oneself, are not two separate entities and, likewise, that there is no difference either between the deity's body and speech, which appear superior, and one's own body and speech, which appear ordinary. On that basis, even on the relative level, one is transformed into and generated as the deity. By training in this, one accomplishes the deity, which is the essence of the result, the purification of delusion. Such is their view.

The three great images are

- the image of the body, which consists of meditating in that manner, visualizing the deity's body with the major and minor marks
- the image of the mind, which consists of meditating on the moon disc in the deity's heart, symbolizing bodhicitta
- the image of speech, the mantra disposed upon the latter

The three objects of concentration refer to the three images.

During the recitation, one must focus on the wisdom deity in front and concentrate on all three images—hence, three objects.

The four branches are the four separate branches of the recitation: namely, the three objects of concentration together with oneself as the meditational deity[27] performing the recitation. These may also be condensed into two objects of concentration, three branches, and so on.[28] Thus, although one is not oneself the deity, one's stream of being is viewed as the deity on account of its one day appearing to be transformed through the causes and conditions.

As an aid to the practice, one meditates on a drawing or statue as the image of the body of whichever deity of the three families one has faith in. One also meditates on the images or symbolic attributes of the mind of the three families, in other words, on the three mudrās—the holding samaya mudrā, the concentration samaya mudrā, and the meditation samaya mudrā. The first of these refers to the vajra and bell held by the practitioner; the second to the symbolic attributes of the wisdom deity's mind, such as the lotus, vajra, sword, and so forth; and the third to the symbolic attributes of the minds of the meditational deity and wisdom deity.[29] Furthermore, there is the image of speech, referring to the recitation. This has three aspects: certainty, uninterruptedness, and completeness. Certainty refers to the performance of the recitation in accordance with the promise one has made. Uninterruptedness refers to the absence of faults during the recitation (yawning, coughing, ordinary conversation, and so forth). And completeness refers to the completion of the number of times the mantra is to be recited.

Then there are the outer requisites. These comprise, above all, one's outer conduct—cleanliness in pure spheres of activity (outer and inner ablutions and so forth), particular times for engaging in the practices, and astrologically auspicious days of the week such as Thursday and lunar mansions such as Puṣyā.[30]

It is held that through the power of bringing together the image of the body, the symbols of the mind, the recitation of the mantra, and the outer requisites, along with the view (the cause) and the outer and inner requisites (the conditions), accomplishment will be attained.

Here, although Padmasambhava indicates separately how, on the ultimate level, everything is devoid of arising and cessation and how, on the relative level, one meditates on the deity, he does not mention how the relative fields of experience are viewed as pure or impure, nor does he mention the particularities of the result. The reason for this is that having said that in relative truth one should meditate that everything is the deity, there is no need for him to say, "In relative truth, view everything as the deity." It is in accordance with how one has established the view that one then trains with concentration. For there should be no conflict between the view and the meditation: it is necessary to have both knowledge and "feet."[31] Another reason is that the secret mantra texts have as their object perfectly pure fields of experience.[32]

The result of the practice is not mentioned separately because although the common activities and accomplishments are not alike, the supreme accomplishment is the same—unsurpassable enlightenment.

2) Presentation of Ubhayatantra

The view of those engaged in the vehicle of Ubhayatantra is that, on the ultimate level, there is no arising or cessation. On this basis, they meditate, on the relative level, on the form body of the deity. By relying on both meditative concentration endowed with four principles and all the other requisite elements, causes, and conditions, they gain accomplishment.

The view of those who have engaged in the vehicle of Ubhayatantra is held to be as follows. On the ultimate level, there is no arising or cessation, and on this basis, they meditate, on the relative level, on the form body of the deity. The expression "meditative concentration endowed with four principles" refers to the principle of one's own nature, the principle of the deity, the principle of concentration, and the principle of recitation. The principle of one's own nature is the visualization of oneself as the meditational deity. The principle of the deity is the invitation of the wisdom deity, who subsequently remains directly in front of one, level with one's brow. The principle of concentration is the arrangement of the moon disc in the heart of the deity visualized in front and in one's own heart while visualizing oneself as the deity, together with the seed syllable encircled by the mantra that is read around it. The principle of recitation is a recitation that is free of the ten faults[33] and combined with one's breath. As one breathes out, one concentrates on the invocation of the deity, and as one breathes in, one concentrates on the bestowal of accomplishments.

By relying on both inner concentration and outer requisites, the coming together of causes and conditions, unimpaired samaya, and so on, one will gain the common accomplishments and the supreme accomplishment: the level of Vajradhara of the four families.

3) Presentation of Yogatantra

a) Brief introduction

> **The view of those engaged in the vehicle of Yogatantra has two aspects—the vehicle of the outer Yogatantra of austerities and the vehicle of the inner Yogatantra of skillful means.**

The view of those who have engaged in the vehicle of Yogatantra, in which one draws closer to the meaning of the ultimate reality,[34] has two aspects. The outer yoga, which is for those who, on the relative level, do not see themselves and the Buddha as equals and who do not undertake the yogic discipline of the conduct in which everything is equal, is the vehicle of tantric austerity. It is so called because, being unable to practice the samayas of "nothing to keep," its practitioners must never part from the common vows,[35] or because, from meditating on the three doors as the three secrets, they will never be influenced by adverse factors.[36] The counterpart of this is the inner yoga, the tantric vehicle of skill in the methods for transforming all that appears into great bliss.

b) Detailed explanation

i) Presentation of the outer Yogatantra

> **The view of those engaged in the vehicle of the outer Yogatantra of austerities is as follows. Rather than emphasizing the outer requisites, they consider the yogic practice to be most important: they meditate on the male and female deities, who on the ultimate level are beyond arising and cessation; and with the concentration of a perfectly pure mind concordant with that view, they meditate, sealed with the four *mudrās*, on the form body of the sublime deity. By this means they gain accomplishment.**

The view of those engaged in the vehicle of the outer Yogatantra of austerities is held to be as follows. Rather than attaching prime importance to outer requisites as in Kriyā, they emphasize the inner yoga, meditating on the male and female deities, whose nature, on the ultimate level, is beyond arising and cessation, and who arise as the appearance aspect. With the concentration of a perfectly pure mind, in which the meditation accords with that view, they meditate on the "form body of the sublime deity." This refers to the deity that is visualized by the samaya holder, who is meditating on the causally compatible deity,[37] associated with both the ultimate deity and the specifically perceived deity[38]—that is, the ultimate deity and the deity of the relative appearance aspect. When training in this, the concentration that makes manifest the way in which the two truths are the nature of the deity is generated by means of the five factors of awakening[39] and the four great miracles[40] and is associated with the four seals, which are as follows.

The great seal of the body (*mahāmudrā*) is the actual body of the deity, and its causal seed syllable, attributes, and so forth. The dharma seal of speech (*dharmamudrā*) is the tongue, which is visualized as a five-pronged vajra and so on. The samaya seal of the mind (*samayamudrā*) comprises concentrating and holding, of which concentrating refers to the aspect of the symbols (the five-pronged vajra and suchlike) of the realization of the five wisdoms and holding refers to the vajra and bell. The action seal of the activities (*karmamudrā*) refers to the emanation of light rays from the crossed vajra on the moon disc in the heart and their reabsorption, inviting the sublime beings, benefiting beings, and so on. With these four seals, the practitioners remain diligent in never deviating from the way of being of the buddhas' body, speech, mind, and activities. An alternative explanation is that they seal them together in a single essence. By training in this manner, putting the emphasis on the inner yoga, they attain the common and supreme accomplishments.

ii) Presentation of the inner Yogatantra

(A) Brief introduction

> **The view of those engaged in the vehicle of the inner Yogatantra of skillful means has three aspects: the method of generation, the method of perfection, and the method of the Great Perfection.**

The view of those engaged in the inner Yogatantra of skillful means has three aspects:

- Mahāyoga, the method of generation, which teaches principally skillful means, the generation of the deity
- Anuyoga, the method of perfection, which teaches predominantly wisdom, the perfection stage
- Ati, the method of the Great Perfection, which teaches mainly their nondual union

(B) Detailed explanation

The detailed explanation is divided into (1) a general explanation of these three methods and (2) a specific explanation of the avenues for applying these.

(1) A general explanation of the three methods

(a) The method of generation

> **In the method of generation, the three concentrations are gradually developed and the maṇḍala is constructed step by step. By meditating in this way, accomplishment is gained.**

In the three inner tantras, it is not the case that the deity is seen when it is generated and not seen when it is not generated, because both cases are similar in that everything is viewed as the spontaneously present maṇḍala of the deity—there is no separation between cause and result. Nevertheless, the fact that one trains by means of concentration implies that the process is something that has to be trained in gradually. For this, all phenomena are viewed as the enlightened state in the reflection-like maṇḍala, which has three aspects: the natural buddha, realizational buddha, and accomplishment buddha. The first refers to sentient beings, and here again there are the buddha of the cause of birth, the buddha of the support of birth, and the buddha of the full manifestation of birth. Of these, the buddha of the cause of birth refers to the three causes that produce the physical body: the sperm, ovum, and mind. The buddha of the support of birth refers to all the physical and mental constituents of both father and mother. The buddha of the full manifestation of birth is the stage of the full formation of one's body. These three are always naturally in the enlightened state.

Second, the realizational buddha refers to beings who dwell on the vidyādhara level. The third, the accomplishment buddha, refers to those who actually behold the ultimate nature. These are also distinguished as natural and situational. Therefore, although there are no nonenlightened phenomena to be seen, this has not been understood and needs be realized. One is not familiar with it and must become so. For this reason, it is held, one trains the mind in the three buddha levels.[41] For this, in order to train the mind to the level of Universal Light, one meditates on the nonconceptual concentration of thusness. To train to the level of the Lotus Endowed, one meditates on the all-illuminating concentration, combining wisdom and compassion. And to train to the level of the Great Wheel of Collections of Letters, one meditates on the concentration of the cause, the seed syllable. These three concentrations are developed in stages. When one gets used to them, one proceeds to construct the maṇḍala of the support and the supported, step by step, and by meditating in this way, accomplishment is attained.

(b) The method of perfection

> **In the method of perfection, on the ultimate level, one never moves from the male and female deities (who on the ultimate level are beyond arising and cessation) and from the expanse of truth, the middle way beyond all concepts. On the relative level, one clearly visualizes the form body of the sublime deity, meditating on everything as the same yet distinct. By this means, one gains accomplishment.**

The method of perfection, Anuyoga, is as follows. All the points that have to be meditated and practiced, as proclaimed in the Yogatantra source texts, are taught from the point of view of one's ability to meditate on everything as clear and complete in the same instant of awareness, whose nature is bodhicitta. They are visualized as one "without moving from the two." While they are inseparably one, they are, in three respects, distinct and unmuddled, appearing like the stars and planets reflected in the ocean, or like the simultaneous display of the four modes of conduct by someone with miraculous powers.[42]

On the ultimate level, there are what are called the two immovabilities. The first is that one does not move from the enlightened knowledge that the whole of phenomenal existence is the nature of the male and female deities in the maṇḍala, which is the reflection of the spontaneously present nature devoid of arising and cessation. The second is that one also does not move from the expanse of truth, the middle way, whose meaning is freedom from every kind of conceptual extreme. And, without moving from these, one meditates, on the relative level, with an enhanced concentration, visualizing all the aggregates, elements, and senses-and-fields as the form body of the sublime deity of the maṇḍala. This is what we call "the single visualization." Whatever arises, whatever one meditates on, everything is the same in ultimate reality, bodhicitta, the expanse devoid of arising and cessation and is therefore described as "inseparably one."

As for the three ways in which the meditation is distinct and unmuddled: first, everything is meditated as the spontaneously present maṇḍala, without any muddling with other concentrations. Second, the visualization of the colors, attributes, and so on, in the maṇḍala of enhanced concentration is unmuddled and distinct. And third, the form of the main deity in the maṇḍala is not mixed up with the other deities. All this is visualized in the same instant of awareness, whose nature is bodhicitta. By meditating in this way, accomplishment is attained.

If one is able to apply this spontaneously and without effort, and one is able to apply it equally in terms of directions and time, it is no different from the Great Perfection. Here, however, the practice is associated with effort, awareness is associated with direction, instants are associated with time, and it is in this sense that all points are completely and instantaneously applied.

In the sections on the generation phase and the perfection phase, apart from the methods for practicing the path, Padmasambhava did not mention any differences in the general view and the result. The reason for this is that they are as he had already explained. In ultimate truth, there is no arising or cessation, and in relative truth, everything is viewed as the illusory, perfectly pure maṇḍala of the deity. The two truths are viewed as inseparable, and the result, unsurpassable enlightenment, is no different from that for the whole of the Great Vehicle. He therefore considered that there was no need to specify them again here.

(c) The method of the Great Perfection

The Great Perfection comprises the meaning (or view)[43] and the method. Of these two, the meaning is that all phenomena are shown as being the nature of enlightenment, self-arisen gnosis. And the method is the means and avenue for its application. The following passage was intended as a brief introduction to these two.

> **In the method of the Great Perfection, one realizes that all phenomena, mundane and supramundane, are inseparable in being, by nature and from the very beginning, the maṇḍala of the enlightened body, speech, and mind. One then meditates on this.**

All the numerous distinctions as this or that, of mundane and supramundane phenomena, relative and ultimate, general and particular characteristics, white and black, and so on, are inseparable—inseparable as the nature of the maṇḍala of the enlightened body, speech, and mind. An analogy can be made with the characteristics of the person and the characteristics of conventional phenomena propounded by ordinary worldly people and the non-Buddhist extremists, which are, all of them, included and described in the Buddhist teachings. In what way are they all inseparable? They are inseparable by their nature from the very beginning. Having realized this, one then trains in this understanding.

After this brief introduction, there is an explanation from the *Guhyagarbha-tantra*, which uses the term "vajra" to indicate the adamantine nature of the enlightened body, speech, and mind:

As it is said in the tantra:

The vajra aggregates
Are known as the five perfect buddhas.
All the many senses-and-fields
Are the maṇḍala of bodhisattvas.
Earth is Locanā, water Māmakī,
Fire is Pāṅḍaravāsinī, wind is Tārā,
And space Dhātvīśvarī.
The three worlds are pure from the beginning.

The meaning of this, as interpreted by the Master,[44] is as follows:

The phenomena of saṃsāra and nirvāṇa are unborn from the beginning, yet they appear in the manner of illusions, capable of functioning, and having the nature, since the beginning, of the ten male and female buddhas and so on.

All the phenomena of saṃsāra and nirvāṇa are the nature of awareness, bodhicitta, and so they are unborn since the beginning. Yet while abiding as the great, unborn emptiness, they appear, and these appearing aspects arise unceasingly. Earth and the rest, which are illusory phenomena capable of performing their respective functions, are, by nature, the ten male and female sugatas, the male and female bodhisattvas, and so on. This does not mean that the elements and so on are thus fabricated or transformed by virtue of the path. It means that they have that nature from the very beginning.

> **All phenomena, therefore, are, by nature, the state of nirvāṇa. The five great elements are, by nature, the five female buddhas. The five aggregates are the buddhas of the five families. The four kinds of consciousnesses are, by nature, four bodhisattvas, and their four objects are, by nature, four beautiful goddesses. The four sense powers are, by nature, four bodhisattvas, and the four times are, by nature, four offering goddesses.**

All phenomena, therefore, are, by nature, the state of nirvāṇa. The five great elements are, by nature, the five female buddhas: earth is the Buddha Locanā, water Māmakī, fire Pāṅḍaravāsinī, wind Samayatārā, and space Dhātvīśvarī. Similarly, the five aggregates are the buddhas of the five families: consciousness is Akṣobhya, feeling Ratnasambhava, perception Amitābha, conditioning factors Amogasiddhi, and form Vairocana. The four consciousnesses are, by nature, four bodhisattvas: the eye consciousness is Kṣitigarbha, the ear consciousness Vajrapāṇi, the nose consciousness Ākāśagarbha, and the tongue consciousness Avalokiteśvara. The four sense objects are, by nature, the four beautiful goddesses that give rise to pleasure in the four consciousnesses: form is the goddess of charm, sound the goddess of song, smell the goddess of garlands, and taste the goddess of dance. The four sense organs are, by nature, four bodhisattvas: the eye organ is Maitreya, the ear Sarvanivāraṇa-viṣkambhin, the nose Samantabhadra, and the tongue Mañjuśrī. The four times are, by nature, the four offering goddesses: the past is the goddess of incense, the present the goddess of flowers, the future the goddess of the lamp, and indeterminate time the goddess of perfumed water.

> **The organ of physical sensation, its related consciousness, its object, and the bodhicitta that arises from them are, by nature, four male wrathful deities. The four extreme views of eternalism, nihilism, and the rest are the four female wrathful deities. The mental consciousness, the adamantine bodhicitta, is, by nature, Samantabhadra. Its objects, phenomena both compounded and uncompounded, are, by nature, Samantabhadrī, matrix of all phenomena.**
>
> **All the things just mentioned have primordially the nature of perfect, manifest buddha. This is not something newly accomplished through the practice of the path.**

The body organ, body consciousness, tangible objects, and the physical sensation (that is, great bliss-bodhicitta) that comes from the latter are the four male wrathful deities. Because the secret vajra of the body organ, on encountering its object, overcomes and nullifies the other sense consciousnesses, these four are classified as the four powerful wrathful deities: physical sensation is Amṛtakuṇḍalin, the body organ that feels is Hayagrīva, the object of sensation is Mahābala, and the consciousness of physical sensation is Yamāntaka.

The four extreme views such as eternalism and nihilism are, by nature, the four female wrathful deities: the pure state of the view of eternalism is the lady of the iron hook; similarly, the view of nihilism is the lady of the lasso, the view of self the lady of the iron chain, and the view of attributes the lady of the bell.

The mind consciousness, the vajra-like indestructible mind whose nature is enlightenment, is, by nature, the Buddha Samantabhadra, the state in which there are never any phenomena to be rejected.[45] The objects of that mind, compounded and uncompounded phenomena, are, by nature, Samantabhadrī, the matrix of all phenomena.

All the above are, by nature, the manifest, perfect enlightened state from the very beginning; they are not something that is newly accomplished by means of the path.

Having commented in this way, drawing from his own textual tradition of tantras, Padmasambhava now cites other compatible scriptures, showing that even though things appear as the three maṇḍalas, their root is bodhicitta, self-arisen gnosis, the single essence:

> **Thus, there are no phenomena, whether compounded or uncompounded (the ten directions, the three times, the three worlds, and so on), that exist separately from one's own mind. As it is said:**

Discerning consciousness, our mind,
Is just the buddhas and the bodhisattvas.
The three worlds are simply this.
The great elements are simply this.

Thus, all compounded and uncompounded phenomena—the ten directions, the three times, the three worlds, and so forth—are none other than one's own mind, as is stated in the *Great Sovereign of Practices, the Victory over the Three Worlds*: "If one realizes, in accordance with one's own unmistaken mind or the power of the mind, that discerning consciousness is the very nature of the buddhas, bodhisattvas, and the like, one is enlightened. If one fails to understand this, everything appears as the vessel and contents that constitute saṃsāra. The three worlds are simply this; the great elements are simply this."

And:

All phenomena abide within the mind.
The mind abides in space.
And space itself has no abode.

And:

All phenomena are by their nature empty.
All phenomena are primordially perfectly pure.
All phenomena are completely radiant.
All phenomena are, by nature, nirvāṇa.
All phenomena are the perfect, manifest state of enlightenment.

Such is the Great Perfection.

As it is said in the *Guhyasamāja-tantra*, "All phenomena abide within the mind." Everything that appears is nothing other than the appearance of one's own mind. And, "The mind itself abides in space." The nature of mind is unborn, like space. "And as for space," it is devoid of all characteristics, so "it does not abide anywhere."

In another scripture too, we read that all phenomena are devoid of established reality and attributes—they cannot be classified in such terms as "They are empty of themselves"; they are by their very nature empty. For all phenomena, the stain of defilements has never, from the very beginning, existed, so they are primordially pure. For all phenomena, the darkness of obscuration has never, from the very beginning, existed, so they are completely radiant. For all phenomena, there have never been either countering factors or antidotes, so they are, by nature, nirvāṇa. All phenomena are free of any diminishing of the two obscurations and of any gathering of the two accumulations, and so they are the manifest state of perfect enlightenment. This is the meaning (or view) of the Great Perfection.

The method of the Great Perfection (marginal note: "great" in the qualities of the result being spontaneously present and in the method for entering that, and "perfection" in that the accumulations of merit and wisdom are perfect and complete) is as follows.

At this point, there is an old annotation in the root text: "The method of the Great Perfection is 'perfection' because the accumulations of merit and wisdom are perfect and complete, and 'great' because the qualities of the result are spontaneously present."

(2) A specific explanation of the avenues for applying the three methods

This comprises an explanation in terms of four methods: (a) four kinds of realization, (b) three characteristics, (c) four branches, and (d) the stages of entering the maṇḍala.

The four kinds of realization are the method of the object, defined as that which is characterized. The three characteristics are the method of skillful means, defined as its characteristics. The four branches of approach and accomplishment are the method of the result, defined as the pith instructions on consummation. And the method of entering the maṇḍala of spontaneous presence is defined as the entrance stage.

Within these, the methods of the single cause and of syllables comprise the method of the object, realization through blessing is the method of skillful means, and direct realization is the method of the result. A similar classification applies to the three characteristics: the characteristic of knowledge is the method of the object, the characteristic of application is the method of skillful means, and the characteristic of the result is the method of the result. Again, for the four stages of approach and accomplishment, the approach is the method of the object, the close approach and accomplishment comprise the method of skillful means, and the great accomplishment is the method of the result. Similarly, for the three stages of entering the maṇḍala, opening the eyes by listening is the method of the object, entering the maṇḍala by familiarization is the method of skillful means, and attaining the great accomplishment by realization through the power of familiarization is the method of the result.

Having got this clear, we come now to the first of these.

(a) The four kinds of realization

> **It is thanks to the path of the four kinds of realization that conviction is gained. The four kinds of realization are (1) the realization that there is a single cause, (2) realization by means of syllables, (3) realization through blessing, and (4) direct realization.**

Whereas the term "perfection" is used in reference to the fact that the two accumulations are perfect and complete, this perfection is not dependent on progress and training as in the case of the lower vehicles. Rather, the enlightened body, speech, and mind are spontaneously present from the very beginning as the qualities of the result, which is why the term "great" is used. The door and means for entering upon that state is the "method," and for this it is necessary to acquire conviction through the path of the four kinds of realization. The four kinds of realization are described in the eleventh chapter of the root tantra as follows:[46]

> A single cause, the method of syllables,
> Blessing, and direct perception—
> With these four kinds of excellent realization,
> Everything is the great king, manifestly perfect.

Accordingly, these are realization that there is a single cause, realization by means of syllables, realization through blessing, and direct realization. These four kinds of realization can be explained both for those who attain realization gradually and for those who do so instantly. Here, however, they are explained in accordance with those who attain the Great Perfection instantly by determining the sole essence, the self-arisen gnosis.

> **First, there is the realization that there is a single cause. Because, on the ultimate level, phenomena are unborn, they are not different from each other. Neither, on the relative level, are they distinct from each other in that they all have the character of illusion. That which is unborn appears in various kinds of displays, as illusory as the moon reflected in water, yet capable of performing functions. These illusions are devoid of essential nature; they are unborn. Thus, the relative and the ultimate are inseparable. This is the realization that there is a single cause.**

In the first place, the realization that there is a single cause (that is, a single nature or basis) is that "all phenomena, on the ultimate level, are unborn" and that they are therefore not different in terms of their unborn nature. Neither are appearances on the relative level distinct from each other, in that they have the character of magical illusions, which are devoid of true existence. This is the accepted viewpoint common to the whole of the Great Vehicle. Despite the fact that it is unborn, that which is unborn appears—like the moon reflected in the water—as a whole variety of pure and impure causes, which are nevertheless able to perform their respective functions.

And illusion-like appearance, even though it appears, is devoid of essential nature—unborn. Therefore, there is no separation between the relative and the ultimate. They are united. The realization that there is a single cause, self-arisen gnosis, is an extraordinary point proclaimed by the most profound scriptures. In short, the essential nature of bodhicitta, self-arisen gnosis, is the indivisible nature of appearance-emptiness, and nothing in the whole of saṃsāra and nirvāṇa lies outside that single way of being, the single cause.

> **Then follows the realization by means of syllables. The unborn nature of phenomena is symbolized by A, the nature of enlightened speech. This unborn nature appears as an illusory display, capable of performing functions and symbolized by O, the nature of the enlightened body. The awareness that realizes this—namely, the illusory gnosis, which is without center or circumference—is symbolized by OM, the nature of the enlightened mind. This is the realization by means of syllables.**

The realization by means of syllables is as follows. This very nature of the inseparability of appearance and emptiness is also shown to be, from the very beginning, the enlightened state, the resultant qualities that are the enlightened body, speech, and mind. The unborn nature of all phenomena is realized as the nature of enlightened speech, symbolized by the letter A. That unborn nature, which appears in the manner of magical illusions, capable of performing functions, is realized as the nature of the enlightened body, symbolized by the letter O (AO).[47] The awareness that realizes this, the illusory gnosis that is without center or circumference, is realized as the nature of the enlightened mind, symbolized by the letter OM (AOM). Furthermore, the wisdom of the primordial union of appearance and emptiness has never had any trace of something to be removed or added; and since it is by nature perfectly pure, saṃsāra is primordially the great enlightened state, while its display abides from the very beginning as the three maṇḍalas. It is this that is realized by means of syllables.

> **The realization that comes about through blessing is the realization that just as the power to "bless" white cotton and make it red is present in madder, so too the power to bless all phenomena as enlightened lies in being blessed by the power of the realization that there is a single cause and of the realization by means of syllables.**

Realization through blessing is the knowledge of the power and blessing of the first two kinds of realization. It is the knowledge and realization that just as the power to "bless" white cotton and make it red is present, for example, in Indian madder,[48] so too the power to bless all phenomena as being primordially enlightened derives from the fact of being blessed by the power of the realization that there is a single cause and of the realization by means of syllables. Of course, all phenomena *are* primordially enlightened, but the fact that they are so is not much help to those who do not have the two realizations. On the other hand, those who do have these two realizations appear to be benefited. Therefore, because it is by the power of these two realizations that all phenomena appear to be blessed as primordially enlightened, we speak of realization through blessing.

> **Finally, there is direct realization through perception. The fact that phenomena abide primordially in the enlightened state does not contradict the scriptures and pith instructions. On the other hand, it is not by relying merely on the words of scriptures and instructions that one attains direct realization. It is gained through conviction in the very depths of one's mind, through one's own awareness.**

Direct realization is as follows. Although in general we have direct perception through the sense faculties and so on, here it is a case of direct perception through the faculty of wisdom, which should be understood as referring to discriminative wisdom. The fact that all phenomena abide primordially in the enlightened state does not in any way contradict the scriptures in which one has confidence or the pith instructions of the lineage masters. Just as one knows from burning, cutting, and rubbing whether something is or is not gold, and whether it is good, flawless gold or flawed gold of poor quality, an analogous examination of the scriptures shows that, on the whole, they do not lead to confusion; and with regard to the various kinds of scriptures (ultimate, expedient, implied, and indirect), confidence is gained by eliminating any flaws in these by means of the pith instructions. Even if one has the scriptures and instructions, one cannot, by simply following the sound of the words, put them into practice in the depth of one's mind. So it is not by relying merely on the words of the scriptures and pith instructions, but by gaining conviction in the very depths of one's mind through one's own awareness or discriminating wisdom, that one attains direct realization. What Padmasambhava is saying is that the scriptures give one an unmistaken understanding of the general points, while the pith instructions prevent one interpreting the intended meanings of the scriptures in any other way, and direct realization gained through wisdom enables one to dispel and resolve the weaknesses in merely listening and so on.

> **Conviction gained through the path is the path of yoga, the actual knowledge of the meaning of the four kinds of realization. This does not depend on the time it takes for the cause to produce a result. Rather, one gains direct realization and conviction oneself.**

The conviction gained through the path in this way is the knowledge and awareness of the meaning of the four kinds of realization, which is the yogic path. This is not a question, as is the case in the vehicle of characteristics, of buddhahood being a result produced from an earlier cause and dependent on time, occurring sometime in the future. Rather, one gains direct realization and conviction oneself, right now, through the faculty of wisdom.

(b) The three characteristics

> **It is thanks to three characteristics that culmination in this is attained. An understanding of the four kinds of realization is the characteristic of knowledge. Repeated familiarization is the characteristic of application. Actualization through the power of such familiarization is the characteristic of the result. These**

> **three characteristics indicate the connection, the requisite, and the ultimate purpose.**

Second, it is through three characteristics—namely, knowledge, application, and actualization—that realization of the meaning of the Great Perfection reaches its culmination. To understand the method of the four kinds of realization, which is what has to be determined, is the characteristic of knowledge—the cause. To familiarize oneself constantly with this is the characteristic of application, which is the condition. To actualize the meaning just as it is by the power of such habituation is the characteristic of the result, the culmination. Here, the causal characteristic of knowledge refers to the view, the conditional characteristic of application refers to meditation, and the characteristic of actualization refers to the result. These three methods enable one to perfect the meaning, and for that reason, they are all indispensable. The three characteristics, then, indicate the connection, the requisite, and the ultimate purpose.

> **"Connection" refers to the causal characteristic of knowledge. This is the realization that all things that are conceptualized as the phenomena of total affliction and complete purity have, from the very beginning, the nature of the enlightened body, speech, and mind. It is the understanding that all phenomena are, by nature, the ultimate expanse of the enlightened state and that this is the meaning of blessing. This knowledge is the connection with the goal, for it is the cause for accomplishing unsurpassable buddhahood.**

"Connection" refers to the causal characteristic of knowledge. It is the direct realization of the meaning of blessing. This comes, on the one hand, through the realization by means of syllables: the understanding that, from the very beginning, all things, conceptualized as the phenomena of total affliction and complete purity, have the nature of the enlightened body, speech, and mind. It also comes from the realization that there is but a single cause—namely, that all phenomena are naturally the expanse of the enlightened state. And this is the meaning of realization through blessing and direct realization. What does this characteristic connect to? It is the cause for accomplishing unsurpassable buddhahood, and thus it connects to the goal.

> **"Requisite" refers to the characteristic of application, that is—the enjoyment in the great sameness, without acceptance or rejection, of all things that are conceptualized as the phenomena of total affliction and complete purity, the five medicines, the five nectars, and so on, for they are primordially the enlightened state. This is a causal factor for accomplishing unsurpassable enlightenment, and it is therefore requisite.**

"Requisite" refers to the characteristic of application—that is, the enjoyment in the great sameness, without acceptance or rejection, of all things, clean and unclean, pure and impure, that are conceptualized as the phenomena of total affliction and complete purity, the five medicines, the five nectars, the five antidotes, the five poisons, and so on. For they are primordially the nature of the enlightened state. Why is such application a requisite? Because it is an exclusive causal factor for accomplishing unsurpassable buddhahood, for there is no way to attain buddhahood without realizing the sameness of acceptance and rejection.

> **"Ultimate purpose" refers to the characteristic of the result, for from the very beginning, all things—the phenomena of total affliction and complete purity and, in particular, the five medicines, five nectars, and so forth—are the enlightened state. They are spontaneously present in the state of great sameness, beyond acceptance and rejection. Therefore samsaric existence itself is, from the beginning, spontaneously present as the characteristic of nirvāṇa, the nature of unsurpassable buddhahood. This actualization of the wheel of inexhaustible ornaments—the enlightened body, speech, and mind—is the ultimate purpose.**

The "ultimate purpose" refers to the characteristic of the result. All the things that are labeled as the phenomena of total affliction and complete purity, in general, and, in particular, the five medicines, five nectars, and so forth, are primordially the enlightened state. They are spontaneously present in the state of great sameness, beyond acceptance and rejection. For this reason, samsaric existence itself is, from the beginning, spontaneously present, and manifest, as the characteristic of nirvāṇa, the nature of unsurpassable buddhahood. Therefore, referring to that which penetrates the minds of those to be trained and slices away all obscuration, the characteristic of the result is the actualization of the wheel of inexhaustible ornaments. This is the enlightened body, speech, and mind, which are perpetually and universally pervasive—the unbounded display of gnosis that fills the expanse of truth, decorating it like a turquoise set in gold. This actualization, then, is the ultimate purpose.

Now one might wonder whether there is not a contradiction between the Great Perfection being primordial buddhahood and its being posited in terms of cause, conditions, and result. The source texts of the lower vehicles—Mahāyoga and so on—hold that the path leads to the accomplishment of the result by way of the four branches of approach and accomplishment. However, in this context, these are not necessary. The four aspects of approach and accomplishment are all complete in the effortless yoga of spontaneous presence, and we therefore apply the pith instruction, the decision that there are in reality no substantial causes, conditions, or results. Thus, in ultimate reality, the nature of bodhicitta, there is no distinction between the object of knowledge, its application, and its actualization: ground and result are inseparable, their nature is the great spontaneous presence.

(c) The four branches

> **For this, one must strive in yogic practice, in which the branches of approach, close approach, accomplishment, and great accomplishment are spontaneously present.**

Third, in relation to the above, one should strive in the yogic practice in which the four branches of approach and accomplishment—namely, the approach, close approach, accomplishment, and great accomplishment—are effortlessly, spontaneously present. This is the general exposition. In the Great Perfection, one needs to apply them in a way that transcends the four stages of approach and accomplishment in Mahāyoga—a way in which all the things comprising cause and result (the elements and aggregates, or the three perfect liberations, or the union of skillful means and wisdom, or the inseparability of appearance and emptiness, and so on) and that appear as aspects of the male and female deities are, by nature, effortlessly and spontaneously present.

> **"Approach" refers to knowledge of bodhicitta. This is the understanding that phenomena are naturally the enlightened state from the very beginning and not made so by the path or contrived as such by means of antidotes.**

In this respect, approach refers to the knowledge of bodhicitta, the ground, which is the union of primordial purity and spontaneous presence. This is the understanding that all the phenomena of total affliction and complete purity are naturally the enlightened state from the very beginning and not newly made so by the path or contrived as such by means of antidotes.

> **"Close approach" refers to the knowledge that we are ourselves the deity. This is the understanding that since all phenomena are, by nature, the enlightened state from the beginning, we too have been the deity, by nature, from the beginning; it is not something that we are accomplishing only now.**

"Close approach" refers to the knowledge, acquired on the basis of that view, that, having the nature of the five aggregates, we are ourselves the deity. This is the understanding that since all phenomena are primordially the nature of the enlightened state, we too are primordially the nature of the deity. It is not that we are made so now in the same way as when, from the state of the view of Mahāyoga and other vehicles, we generate the visualization of ourselves as the deity.

> **"Accomplishment" refers to the generation of the female deities. This is the understanding that from the expanse of space, the Great Mother, space itself appears in the form of the four great mothers—earth, water, fire, and wind—and that they are, from the beginning, the mothers that perform all activities.**

"Accomplishment" refers to the generation of the female deities. Here again, this is not like generating the female deity in Mahāyoga and other vehicles. Rather, from the expanse of space, the Great Mother, space itself arises as the four great mothers—earth, water, fire, and wind. This, then, is the understanding that these are, from the beginning, the mothers that perform the activities of creating space, supporting, bringing together, ripening, and moving.

> **"Great accomplishment" refers to the interconnection of skillful means and wisdom. From the primordial union of the wisdoms of the five great mothers and the five aggregates (the fathers of all the buddhas appearing without expectancy from the emptiness-space of the mother), bodhicitta manifests in the form of the male and female bodhisattvas.**

"Great accomplishment" refers to the interconnection of skillful means and wisdom. In what way are they connected? From the female buddhas (wisdom, the absence of intrinsic existence in the five great elements) and the space of the mother (emptiness, perfect liberation), the male deities (skillful means), buddhas of the five aggregates, appear unobstructedly, free of expectancy. It is not that they are united now, by means of the path—they are united from the very beginning. From their union, which is the nature of inseparability as bodhicitta, all the senses-and-fields arise as the male and female bodhisattva manifestations.[49] This is not as when, in Mahāyoga and the other vehicles, the sons and daughters emanate from the bodhicitta of the male and female deities in union, but that their nature is, from the very beginning, the enlightened state.

> **Within the state of primordial enlightenment, illusion delights in illusion, and at the moment of bliss in the illusory stream of supreme bliss, the absence of all characteristics equal to space beyond all reference is fully realized and is spontaneously present. The four demons are subdued and the ultimate goal is achieved.**

Within that state, the illusion-like male deity, the gnosis of awareness, delights in the sense object, the illusion-like female deity, the expanse of truth. And in that, the wisdom of bliss—unobstructed, nonconceptual, inseparable, free of all bias—manifests in every way, experiencing realization just like the playing of music. There is not even an atom's worth of dualistic clinging. Consequently, the delighting wisdom is supreme bliss on account of the way in which one sports in the illusory stream of such bliss and experiences it. The timeless continuum of the essential nature is like space. At the very moment of bliss, the sole self-arisen wisdom, the ultimate nature of phenomena—the meaning of the door of perfect liberation that is the absence of attributes, free of all elaborations, beyond all reference to any limits, equal to space, and that does not go beyond the fence of the great equanimity—is fully realized and is spontaneously present without any effort to produce it. Dualistic grasping, the cause of tainted phenomena, is purified as self-arisen wisdom, and the unceasing stream of the essential nature appears, accumulating merit. The absence of even the slightest clinging to elaborations and attributes accumulates wisdom. The spontaneous accomplishment of these two accumulations, this great self-arisen wisdom, subdues the four kinds of demons and achieves the final goal.

The manner in which the four demons are subdued is as follows. With the approach branch, the concentration of the unborn, which is characterized by the knowledge of bodhicitta, overcomes the demon of the lord of death. With close approach, the illusion-like concentration, which is characterized by the knowledge that one is oneself the deity, overcomes the demon of the aggregates. With the accomplishment branch, the undefiled concentration, which is characterized by the generation of the female deity, overcomes the demon of the defilements. And with the great accomplishment, the concentration that is beyond all reference and equal to space, and which is characterized by the union of skillful means and wisdom, overcomes the demon "child of the gods," the demon of distracting interruptions. Thus, the path that has the power to enable one to overcome the four demons is the perfectly pure path—that is, the great path of spontaneous accomplishment without effort.

(d) The four stages of entering the maṇḍala

All phenomena are perfectly pure from the beginning and are a maṇḍala beyond all dimension, a vast and measureless palace that grants every wish. To enter this primordial, unsurpassable maṇḍala, one must open one's eyes, which is achieved by hearing the texts of the vehicles of skillful means. To understand their meaning is to behold the maṇḍala. To gain familiarity, once one has understood, is to enter the maṇḍala. And when, once entered, the maṇḍala becomes manifest, the great accomplishment is attained.

The procedure for entering the maṇḍala of the Great Perfection does not depend, as it does in the lower vehicles, on efforts such as constructing or laying out a maṇḍala. It is the magical display of all phenomena, perfectly pure from the very beginning, that constitutes the maṇḍala of the measureless palace, unbounded by spatial and temporal demarcations and granting every possible wish. The entrance to this primordial, unsurpassable maṇḍala, which is completely beyond the realm of such things as colored powders and images, consists, first of all, in the wisdom that comes from listening, through hearing from one's teacher the texts of the Great Perfection and the other vehicles of skillful means.[50] These texts, such as the thirteenth chapter of the *Guhyagarbha-tantra*, together with the pith instructions, engender an understanding of the meaning of primordial buddhahood. Through listening in this way, one's eyes are opened. To understand the meaning of these texts, using the wisdom that comes from reflection, is to see the maṇḍala. To gain familiarity with it on the basis of one's understanding, using the wisdom that comes from meditation, is to enter the maṇḍala—that is, to receive empowerment. And when, once entered, the maṇḍala becomes manifest, the great accomplishment is attained.

> **This method is the culmination, the Great Perfection. The level of the Great Wheel of Collections of Syllables is spontaneously entered. Beings with the sharpest faculties have understood that primordial enlightenment means that they have been enlightened from the very beginning, and they progress powerfully on the path. Their actions are not the actions of ordinary beings.**

This section of Padmasambhava's text was taught in order to show that this method of the Great Perfection is the most exclusive of all. This method is the culmination of all the causal and resultant vehicles. It is the Great Perfection, the state of perfect equality. There is no progressing higher than that. The result of this path is the entrance, effortlessly and spontaneously, into the level of the Great Wheel of Collections of Syllables.

Generally speaking, in the vehicle of characteristics, the level of buddhahood is usually referred to as "Universal Light," because, through the emanation of numerous rays of light, it turns beings to be trained into suitable vessels. In the Diamond Vehicle, there are usually said to be three levels of buddhahood. Universal Light is the dharmakāya, devoid of attributes, naturally pervading everything with radiant light. The Lotus Endowed is the ground of unattached compassion, the state in which nonconceptual wisdom sees the meaning of the dharmakāya, even though there is nothing to be seen. With regard to the Great Wheel of Collections of Syllables, at that very moment, the nature of the maṇḍala of wisdoms and attributes is effortlessly and spontaneously accomplished. "Syllables" in this context refers to two things: wisdoms and attributes; and attributes are again subdivided into two: name and form. Form is also twofold, appearing completely or partially. The spontaneously present Great Wheel of Collections of this maṇḍala of resultant qualities is referred to both as the level of the Great Wheel of Collections of Syllables and as the thirteenth level, the level of buddhahood.

Regarding this, beings with the sharpest mental faculties have understood that the primordial enlightened state means that they have been enlightened from the very beginning, and in an instant, without their depending on the effortful activities of the path, their familiarity with this grows in power: their progress is instantaneous and has nothing to do with the efforts in reflection and familiarization that ordinary beings make.

However much ordinary people may hear and reflect on this, they will not gain confidence in its truth and profundity. Since it is difficult to have confidence and to understand it with their ordinary minds and they do not recognize how true and profound it is, they judge by their own experience and think it is the same for everyone. "It's all a pack of lies," they say,

belittling superior beings and giving rise to an attitude of repudiation. This is why this teaching is extremely secret and also why it is called the Secret Vehicle.

However much ordinary beings may hear and earnestly reflect on such points, they will not gain confidence in the truth and extreme profundity of this teaching. Because it is difficult for them to gain confidence and to understand it with their ordinary minds and they do not recognize its truth and profundity, they judge by their own experience and imagine that everyone else's experience is the same. They think that it is completely false to say that all—those who have realized the Great Perfection and all phenomena—are enlightened from the very beginning. Thus they belittle beings of superior faculties and give rise to an attitude of repudiation with regard to the Great Vehicle. For this reason, this teaching needs to be kept extremely secret, and this is why the Teacher[51] himself referred to it as the "Secret Vehicle."

Therefore, until their disciples have understood that all phenomena are primordially the enlightened state, teachers use the lower vehicles to benefit beings; and to avoid wasting those beings' potential, they should be well versed in the defects of saṃsāra, the qualities of nirvāṇa, and all the vehicles. Disciples should not be guided by a teacher who is ignorant of some aspects. All this has been extensively taught.

So until their disciples develop the intellectual capacity to understand fully the fact that all phenomena are primordially the enlightened state, teachers use the lower vehicles to benefit beings through the paths of the gods and humans, listeners, solitary realizers, and so on, and thus do not waste the spiritual potential of their disciples. For this reason, there are extensive passages in the sūtras and tantras mentioning that for disciples of mean intelligence, the master should be well versed in the defects of saṃsāra, the praises of the qualities of nirvāṇa, and all the stages of all the different vehicles and should instruct them on these points one by one in accordance with the disciples' experience. And the disciples, for their part, should not be guided by teachers who are ignorant of some aspects of the different vehicles.

B. An explanation of the different kinds of yogic disciplines

1. Brief introduction

> **Along with the different views, there are also specific kinds of spiritual training and yogic discipline. Those who have no spiritual training are the unreflective and the nihilistic extremists. Those who have a spiritual training display four kinds of practices: the mundane trainings of the materialists and eternalistic extremists, the spiritual training of the listeners, the spiritual training of the bodhisattvas, and the unsurpassable spiritual training.**

Because of the differences between the above views, different resultant qualities are desired, and so there are also different specific forms of physical training[52] and yogic disciplines or practices for transforming the practitioner's way of being from its former condition. Whatever the view determines (like an eye), the spiritual training and yogic discipline follow (like the feet).

On account of the differences between the views, there may or may not be any spiritual trainings. There are two views that are not associated with spiritual training: those of worldly unreflective beings and of the non-Buddhist nihilistic extremists. The reason for this is that their views do not imply anything that needs to be accomplished.

Those views that are associated with spiritual training, on account of the fact that they do imply something to be accomplished, are of four kinds. First, there are the trainings of the worldly materialists and non-Buddhist eternalistic extremists, who undertake mundane practices unconnected with the path to liberation. Then there are the spiritual training of the listeners and that of the bodhisattvas: both of these constitute supramundane paths. Finally, there is the unsurpassable spiritual training.

2. Detailed explanation

> **The unreflective are ignorant with regard to the karmic law of cause and effect, and they do not, therefore, engage in spiritual training. Neither do the nihilistic extremists, for they have nihilistic views. The materialists, in order to achieve advantage in this life, engage in practices such as ritual cleanliness. The eternalistic extremists, in order to purify the self that they believe exists, indulge mistakenly in austerities, such as the**

mortification of the body and the ordeal of five fires, and in yogic disciplines.

As mentioned above in the context of their view, worldly unreflective beings are ignorant with regard to causes and results, and so they know nothing about what they should adopt and avoid. They therefore follow no spiritual training. The non-Buddhist nihilistic extremists have a view that denies cause and result, so they are not interested in any benefit for future lives. Consequently, they likewise undertake no spiritual discipline. These two groups are destitute of any kind of spiritual practice.

As for those who follow a spiritual training, the mundane materialists have practices such as ritual cleanliness in order to acquire power, cattle, and other means that give them superiority over others in this life. The non-Buddhist eternalistic extremists, in order to purify the permanent self that they believe exists, indulge mistakenly in meaningless hardships—austerities such as enduring the torment of five fires (four fires at the cardinal points and the sun above), wearing their body down through exposure to heat and cold, and other such ordeals—and also in base yogic disciplines such as acting like a dog or pig.

The disciplines of the listeners are described in the Vinaya:

Abandon every evil deed,
Practice virtue well
And perfectly subdue your mind:
This is Buddha's teaching.

> **The listeners consider that positive and negative phenomena exist on both the relative and ultimate levels, and they follow the spiritual training and yogic discipline of implementing virtue and avoiding negativity.**

Regarding the listeners' spiritual training, the Vinaya gives the following summary of the three trainings:

> Abandon every evil deed.

This refers to the training in discipline, which is the contrary of the path of the ten nonvirtuous actions, in particular wrong actions such as the four extremely grave actions that count as radical defeats: killing, taking that which is not given, sexual misconduct, and telling lies.

> Practice virtue well.

This corresponds to the training in wisdom—the sublime path that is to be followed and the resultant qualities that are to be attained, all of which are contained in the wisdom that is the unmistaken realization of the meaning of the four truths.

> And perfectly subdue your mind.

This refers to the training of the mind[53]—that is, turning away from outer distractions and training in the concentration of one-pointed meditative equipoise.

This is the Buddha's teaching.

This last line validates the verse as authoritative. Unlike the non-Buddhist scriptures such as those of Īśvara, it is true and can be trusted by everyone, for it was taught by the Buddha; it is the holy Dharma, the excellently spoken Vinaya.

In accordance with this, the listeners consider that all positive and negative phenomena exist on both the relative and ultimate levels, meaning that any phenomena that appear to the relative consciousness also appear to the ultimate consciousness, so that they exist on both levels. Therefore, with their bodies and speech, they follow the spiritual training and yogic discipline of implementing virtue and avoiding nonvirtue.[54]

Earlier, in the section on the view, the solitary realizers were presented separately, but here their spiritual training is not mentioned because it is similar to that of the listeners.

The spiritual training of the bodhisattvas is described in *The Vows of a Bodhisattva*:

> **Failure to benefit as circumstances dictate,**
> **Failure to use miraculous powers to intimidate and so on—**
> **Such faults are absent in those whose intentions are virtuous,**
> **For they are filled with compassion and love.**[55]

Whatever bodhisattvas do, positive or negative, if they are imbued with great compassion, they will not damage their vows. For, the bodhisattva vow, in brief, is to act on the basis of great compassion.

The bodhisattvas' spiritual training is described next. In order to liberate all sentient beings from the ocean of saṃsāra, they cultivate the intention to attain the wisdom of omniscience. This is the main body of their vows. But until they attain that wisdom of omniscience, they are unable to benefit beings, so if they are to attain it, three things are indispensable: the cause, which is bodhicitta; the root, which is compassion; and the consummation, which is skill in means. The factors that counteract these, and which are naturally shameful deeds[56] for bodhisattvas, are their four radical defeats—namely, giving up bodhicitta (which is contrary to taking hold of bodhicitta); failure to protect sentient beings out of stinginess; maliciously harming beings (these last two faults being incompatible with compassion); and abandoning the holy Dharma, which is contrary to skill in means. If they are free of these four factors and are imbued with compassion, bodhisattvas also need to act physically and verbally to subjugate beings. As we find in the *Twenty Verses on the Vows of a Bodhisattva*, failure to act for beings' welfare by employing subjugating activities, when these are appropriate as a means for training beings, will cause a bodhisattva's vow to deteriorate. And failure to tame beings by the seemingly ignoble use of miraculous displays to trick, abuse, or intimidate them, and so on, will also lead to a deterioration of the vow. Why is this? Because of their loving and compassionate attitude, bodhisattvas' intentions are virtuous, so even if they act harshly, they are without fault.[57] Provided they are imbued with the motivation of great compassion, whatever they do, whether virtuous or seemingly negative, none of their activities will damage the bodhisattva vow. To sum up, the bodhisattva vow is to act on the basis of great compassion.

The unsurpassable training is described in the *Sūtra of the Great Samaya*:

> **In those who have the utmost certainty with regard to**
> **Buddha's vehicle,**
> **Even indulgence in all five defilements and sense**
> **pleasures**
> **Will be the very height of discipline,**
> **As unstained as lotus petals unsullied by the mud.**

The spiritual training of the unsurpassable secret is as mentioned in the *Sūtra of the Great Samaya*. In those whose minds have the fullest certainty or assurance with regard to the Buddha's vehicle—the unsurpassable great sameness of skillful means and wisdom—even indulging in all the five defilements and five sense pleasures leaves no stain. They are like lotus petals unsullied by the mud. For such sublime individuals, the whole of the listeners' discipline and the bodhisattvas' vows will be perfect and complete.

All phenomena are in the state of sameness from the beginning, so compassion is not something to be cultivated and anger is not something to be eschewed. This does not mean, however, that compassion does not arise for those who fail to understand.

Because all phenomena are in the state of sameness from the beginning, we have compassion from the very beginning; it is impossible to be separated from it, and it is not something to be cultivated. And since anger is devoid of specific characteristics, it is not something to be abandoned. The intended meaning of this passage is that because everything is in the state of sameness from the very beginning, if one is imbued with this understanding of sameness, there is never any transgression.

To sum up, with regard to conduct, the listener's vow involves the avoidance of deeds that harm sentient beings. The bodhisattva vow involves, in addition, the implementation of activities that benefit beings. And the vows of the secret mantras involve, as well as these first two, the practice of the activities of the tathāgatas. Furthermore, regarding the relationship between mental states and actual deeds, in the case of the listeners' vows, the greatest importance is ascribed to the actions themselves. In the case of the bodhisattva vows, compassion is the principal concern. And in the case of the secret mantras, wisdom is paramount. Again, the listeners follow the example of the sublime arhats of the past, bodhisattvas follow the example of the sublime bodhisattvas who abide on the great levels, and those practicing the secret mantras follow the example of the tathāgatas themselves.

The sameness of phenomena may have been realized, but this does not mean that compassion does not arise for those who have never realized this or for those practicing the eight vehicles who have only partially done so: nonconceptual compassion, by its very nature, arises spontaneously.

> **And to the extent that, as far as one's view is concerned, one has realized primordial perfect purity, one's spiritual training and yogic discipline will also be perfectly pure.**

In short, regarding the samaya of the great sameness in the Secret Mantra Vehicle, there is absolutely nothing in the whole of the practice that is impure. To the extent that one realizes the view that things are perfectly pure from the very beginning, one's spiritual training and yogic discipline will also be practiced in a manner that is perfectly pure. This last sentence was written as a further summary of the Mantra Vehicle's samaya of the great sameness, showing how it differs from the spiritual trainings and yogic disciplines of the lower vehicles.

III. Conclusion

A. The disciples for whom these instructions were intended

> **Like those born blind who spontaneously gain their sight,**
> **If there are superior beings**
> **Who hold the power of wisdom and skillful means,**
> **May they encounter this secret Garland of Views.**

The secret teaching entitled *A Garland of Views* (so called because it arranges in a continuous sequence, like a garland, the different views, higher and lower, and summarizes their purpose) brings together in a few words the meaning of all the vehicles, in the form of a pith instruction that is easy to remember. In a few words, it enables us to understand many important points, and in this respect, it is like a shining lamp. Yet it is something that should be kept secretly hidden away, like a precious jewel, or, according to another explanation, it should be kept secret through the skillful means of great compassion, for the view of the Great Perfection is the most exclusive of all.

Just as there are people born blind who cannot see anything but who, thanks to their merit, one day chance upon a precious jewel or naturally gain their sight, there are, likewise, beings who, blinded by ignorance from beginningless time, have never seen the truth and who nevertheless, because of their former merits, meet a spiritual master, through whom they gain the eyes of the three wisdoms and discover or come to hold the power of wisdom and skillful means, thus becoming vessels for the teachings of the natural Great Perfection. It was for supreme beings like these that Padmasambhava made the prayer that they may meet with this profound teaching, whose meaning is contained in this precious instruction.

B. Colophon marking the completion of the text

This completes the pith instruction entitled *A Garland of Views*.

This completes the pith instruction entitled *A Garland of Views*, which was composed by the great master Padmasambhava when he was about to leave Tibet. He composed it for King Trisong Detsen and other disciples in a meadow at the Peacock Lake of Trakmar, after he had sung three songs at the time of their parting homage.[58]

By the merit of my writing this,
May I, in this and all my lives to come,
Enter the vajra heart of Padma Mañjuśrī,

And understanding all the deep and crucial points of the
perfect view,
May I, for beings, shine light upon the Buddha's excellent path.
I, Mipham, wrote this at a single sitting. Mangalam.[59]

These original notes of Jamgön Mawa'i Senge Mipham Ösel Dorje, embellished with the structural outline from the commentary by the Lord of Secrets, Lodrö Thaye, were copied out during the "Goal Fulfilling" year, the female earth sheep year of the fifteenth sixty-year cycle (1919), in the mountain retreat at Shechen. They were corrected and finalized by the great holder of the piṭakas, Khenchen Lama Kunzang Pelden.

The pith instructions, distilled essence of the conquerors' and
vidyādharas' lineages,
Were retained in the ocean of Padmasambhava's mind
And offered as instructions to the retinue of fortunate
ministers—
A cherished jewel for those who hold the Buddha's teachings.

Even at the end of time, the fresco of the aspiration
Born in the supreme protector's mind remains unspoiled.
Why then should those who hold the blessings of the short
lineage
Not have the fortune to enjoy this nectar?

For them, I humbly copied out the Jamgön Lama's notes
Without, I think, corrupting them with my own ideas.
Any errors I have made are through the defects of my
  intellect—
Please forgive them, you who have the Dharma eye!

This was written by Jamyang Lodrö Gyamtso.[60] May virtue ensue!

Notes

Translator's Introduction

1. For a discussion on the development of the ways in which the tantra vehicles were classified, see Jacob Dalton, "A Crisis of Doxography: How Tibetans Organized Tantra during the 8th–12th Centuries." *Journal of the International Association of Buddhist Studies* 28, no. 1 (2005): 115–81.

Commentary by Jamgön Mipham

1. Tib. *rnal 'byor chen po*. Mipham Rinpoche's use of the Tibetan term here is probably deliberate. While its Sanskrit equivalent would be "Mahāyoga," the term "Mahāyoga" did not have the same meaning in the eighth century as it came to have later in the nine-vehicle system accepted by the Nyingmapas, where it is almost always referred to by the Tibetan phoneticization of the Sanskrit name rather than the Tibetan translation. In the system of the four tantric vehicles adopted by the followers of the New Translations, *rnal 'byor chen po* can refer to Anuttarayoga, but this would not be an appropriate translation here. We have therefore chosen to translate it literally into English as "Great Yoga."

2. Tib. *legs pa'i yon tan drug*, the six qualities of the greatness of a buddha (bhagavān): perfection of mastery, perfection of form, perfection of glory, perfection of renown, perfection of wisdom, and perfection of diligence.

3. The structure of this passage in the Tibetan leads us to suspect a scribal error, resulting in the omission of this third item, which may or may not

have had a marginal note. We have taken the liberty to insert it for the sake of clarity.

4. This is a gloss of the Sanskrit term *tīrthika* (Tib. *mu stegs pa*), which, as explained below, is used generally to signify non-Buddhist proponents of nihilism and eternalism, but in this text signifies the proponents of eternalism, which is considered by Buddhists to be an extreme view.

5. Lit. "words like *sandhapa*." Mipham Rinpoche is referring to a word of Indian origin, which appears to have any number of meanings, depending on the context, much in the same way as the word "things" is used in English to refer to whatever is necessary or appropriate. Mipham is simply stressing the point that the term "materialist" has a quite specific meaning in this text.

6. To avoid confusion with the general use of the terms and their specific use in this text, we have rendered them, in the sections that follow, as "nihilistic extremists" and "eternalistic extremists."

7. Tib. *'jig tshogs la lta ba*, the view whereby the five aggregates, which are transitory and composite, are regarded as a permanent, independent, and single "I" and "mine." This view is the basis of all other wrong views.

8. The view presented here is that of the Sāṃkhya. For more detailed information on this and the other non-Buddhist philosophical schools presented here, see Shantarakshita, *The Adornment of the Middle Way*, trans. Padmakara Translation Group (Boston: Shambhala Publications, 2005), and Jamgön Kongtrul, *The Treasury of Knowledge: Book Six, Parts One and Two: Indo-Tibetan Classical Learning and Buddhist Phenomenology*, trans. Gyurme Dorje (Boston: Snow Lion, 2012).

9. Tib. *dbang phyug*, Skt. *Īśvara*.

10. This is the Vaiśeṣika view.

11. This third view of eternalistic extremists is that of the Vedānta.

12. This is an explanation of the Sanskrit word *bodhisattva*, which was trans-

lated into Tibetan as *byang chub sems dpa'*, lit. "enlightenment hero" or "enlightenment being."

13. The basis of appearance (Tib. *snang gzhi*) refers to the thing on which an appearance or perception is based. The sight of a rope gives rise to the perception of a rope or a snake or anything else one might perceive, depending on the conditions. Similarly, an unenlightened person's mental and physical components constitute the basis for that person's perception of himself or herself as an "I."

14. The Tibetan word *'phags pa* (Skt. *āryā*) generally means "sublime" or "elevated," though in the context of the four truths, it is commonly translated as "noble." See also glossary s.v. "sublime being."

15. The number of degrees of defilement that are eliminated by those who attain the level of stream-enterer appears to be variable. Some stream-enterers have eliminated the fifth degree of defilement, others have eliminated the fourth and then, on eliminating the fifth, become candidates for the state of once-returner. By eliminating the sixth, they become once-returners abiding by the result. See Longchen Yeshe Dorje, Kangyur Rinpoche, *Treasury of Precious Qualities*, bk. 1, trans. Padmakara Translation Group (Boston: Shambhala Publications, 2010), 230, and Jamgön Kongtrul, *The Treasury of Knowledge: Book Six, Part Three: Frameworks of Buddhist Philosophy*, trans. Elizabeth M. Callahan (Ithaca, N.Y.: Snow Lion Publications, 2007), 142–44.

16. According to the Abhidharma, in which the mind is treated as a sense organ, there are eighteen constituents (Tib. *khams bco brgyad*), comprising six sense organs (eye, ear, nose, tongue, body, and mind), six sense objects (forms, sounds, smells, tastes, physical sensations, and mental objects), and six corresponding sense consciousnesses. Of these, the ten constituents with form (Tib. *gzugs can gyi khams bcu*) comprise the first five sense organs and their five objects, as do the ten senses-and-fields (or *āyatanas*) with form (Tib. *gzugs can gyi skye mched bcu*). To these are added certain mental objects that are considered, in the Abhidharma, to have form and that are termed "imperceptible form" (Tib. *rnam par rig byed min pa'i gzugs*). All these are included in the aggregate of form

(Tib. *gzugs kyi phung po*). See also Longchen Yeshe Dorje, *Treasury of Precious Qualities*, bk. 1, appendix 4.

17. Tib. *dkar po rnam par mthong ba'i sa*, the first of the eight levels in the Basic Vehicle, corresponding to the listeners' path of accumulation; the stage at which, for the first time, one perceives the virtuous qualities of complete purity.

18. Of the twelve links of dependent origination, consciousness, name-and-form, sense powers, contact, feeling, birth, and aging-and-death are related to suffering; ignorance, craving, and grasping are related to the defilements; and conditioning factors and becoming are related to karma. For a detailed account of the twelve links, see Longchen Yeshe Dorje, *Treasury of Precious Qualities*, bk. 1, 175.

19. "Total affliction" (Tib. *kun nas nyon mongs pa*) refers collectively to the truth of suffering and the truth of the origin. See glossary.

20. The cause of the Bodhisattva Vehicle is bodhicitta, the mind set on supreme enlightenment, and bodhisattvas are those who have that bodhicitta. In the present context, the terms "Bodhisattva Vehicle," "vehicle of the transcendent perfections," and "vehicle of characteristics" are synonymous.

21. Correct relative truth (Tib. *yang dag pa'i kun rdzob*) covers all things that are conventionally designated as being "true" by ordinary people (though their perceptions are, of course, deluded with regard to the ultimate nature of phenomena). Such things are also perceived as capable of performing their respective functions. Mistaken relative truth (Tib. *log pa'i kun rdzob*), on the other hand, covers those things that ordinary people generally consider to be false and that are incapable of performing functions. An example of correct relative truth is a lake, which by common consensus contains water, which in turn has the functions or properties of moistening and quenching thirst. By contrast, a mirage contains no water and cannot quench a desert traveler's thirst. It is therefore classified as mistaken relative truth.

22. Tib. *snang tsam po*—that is, ordinary appearances.

23. The ten strengths, four fearlessnesses, and other qualities of a buddha's realization. See Longchen Yeshe Dorje, *Treasury of Precious Qualities*, bk. 1, appendix 5.

24. Lit. "for them it would be an unjustified negation to say that phenomena like the aggregates do not exist at all."

25. In other words, the principle of one's own nature refers to maintaining the Madhyamaka view of emptiness.

26. The six deities are the deity as emptiness, deity as letter, deity as sound, deity as form, deity as mudrā, and deity as symbol. See Longchen Yeshe Dorje, *Treasury of Precious Qualities*, bk. 2, 101 and 375n77.

27. Tib. *dam tshig sems dpa'*, Skt. *samayasattva*.

28. Other texts may mention two objects of concentration, three branches, and so on, in which case, they include all the above.

29. Tib. *ye shes sems dpa'*, Skt. *jñānasattva*.

30. Puṣyā is the eighth of the twenty-eight lunar mansions in Indian astrology.

31. Tib. *rig pa dang rkang pa ldan pa*. In his commentary on the *Sūtra of Mindfulness of the Three Jewels*, Mipham Rinpoche explains that "knowledge" is synonymous with "sight" and corresponds to right view, while "feet" corresponds to the other aspects of the noble eightfold path, the path of meditation.

32. In other words, pure vision is an essential feature of the tantric path.

33. The ten faults in mantra recitation, as listed in the tantra *The Wheel of Fearful Wisdom Lightning*, are reciting too loudly or too softly, too quickly or too slowly, too forcefully or too leisurely, corrupting the syllables, distractions, interruptions from yawning and so on, and wandering thoughts.

34. Tib. *chos nyid kyi don la reg pa*, lit. "one touches the ultimate nature (of phenomena)."

35. Beings who are able to practice the four samayas of "nothing to keep" are practitioners of the Great Perfection with the very highest degree of realization, who are able to abide continually in ultimate reality. Practitioners without that capacity need to observe scrupulously the common vows and commitments. See Longchen Yeshe Dorje, *Treasury of Precious Qualities*, bk. 2, 205–8.

36. The Tibetan term *thub pa rgyud kyi theg pa* (vehicle of tantric austerity) is here explained in terms of different meanings of the word *thub pa*, referring, in the first place, to the austerities (*dka' thub*) of keeping vows strictly and, in the second, to the ability to face up to adverse conditions by meditating on oneself as the deity.

37. Tib. *rgyu mthun pa'i lha*. The deity visualized by the practitioner is not the actual deity but in being similar to the latter, acts as the cause for realizing the deity.

38. Tib. *sems pa'i bye brag gi lha*, the specific deity (for example, one of the buddhas of the three families) that is chosen according to the particular mental inclinations and perceptions of the practitioner.

39. Tib. *mgon par byang chub pa lnga*. The five factors are emptiness, the moon throne, seed syllable, hand implements, and body of the deity.

40. Tib. *cho 'phrul chen po bzhi*. The four great miracles are concentration, blessing, empowerment, and offering.

41. Further mention of these three buddha levels is made on pp. 86–87.

42. The four modes of conduct (Tib. *spyod lam bzhi*) are walking, standing, sitting, and lying down.

43. Tib. *don*.

44. "The Master" here refers to Guru Padmasambhava.

45. Tib. *thams cad du dor bya'i chos med pa*. This is an explanation of Samantabhadra's name, "Universal Good." If there were anything to be rejected or discarded (that is, something bad), this state of buddhahood would not be, in every respect, good.

46. *Guhyagarbha-tantra*, chap. 11, verse 2. See also Longchen Yeshe Dorje, *Treasury of Precious Qualities*, bk. 2, appendix 3, p. 347, and Jamgön Kongtrul, *The Treasury of Knowledge: Book Six, Part Four: Systems of Buddhist Tantra*, trans. Elio Guarisco and Ingrid McLeod (Ithaca, N.Y.: Snow Lion Publications, 2005), 317.

47. Though pronounced "o," this letter in Sanskrit and Tibetan is a compound formed by the addition of the *o* vowel sign to the basic letter *a*. The further addition of *m* creates the compound letter OM (AOM). All three letters therefore share the same basic letter *a*.

48. Tib. *btsod*, the plant *Rubia cordifolia*, whose roots contain a red dye, used since antiquity for dyeing textiles.

49. Rongzom Paṇḍita explains this succinct passage as indicating the connection between the three elements in each of three series: (a) skillful means, wisdom, and bodhicitta; (b) the father, mother, and sons and daughters; and (c) the three doors of perfect liberation: emptiness, absence of attributes (which is explained in the next passage), and absence of expectancy.

50. The vehicles of skillful means are Mahāyoga, Anuyoga, and Atiyoga.

51. Tib. *ston pa*, referring to Buddha Śākyamuni.

52. Tib. *dka' thub*, variously translated as "ascetic practice," "austerities," and so forth, refers in this context not simply to different kinds of mortification but to the whole range of practices that involve a degree of self-discipline and effort.

53. Tib. *sems kyi bslab pa*, also known as the training in concentration (*ting nge 'dzin gyi bslab pa*).

54. Because the listeners understand the Buddha's teachings as presenting things as if they existed truly, they believe in the true existence of positive and negative actions and therefore practice accordingly.

55. As will be explained below, in order to prevent others from doing great evil, bodhisattvas may resort to harsh means and miraculous powers.

If they fail to do so when necessary, they are committing the last two of the forty-six secondary downfalls.

The final two lines of this verse can be read in two ways. On the one hand, bodhisattvas are free of the faults of failing to subjugate beings when necessary. On the other hand, when they do use harsh means to subjugate beings, they are not at fault because they are performing such apparently negative deeds out of compassion and love, and their intentions are entirely virtuous.

56. Shameful deeds (lit. "that cannot be mentioned" or "cannot be praised") cover all kinds of wrongdoing and are of two sorts—those that are naturally negative (Tib. *rang bzhin gyi kha na ma tho ba*), such as the ten nonvirtuous actions, and those that involve breaches of vows (Tib. *bcas pa'i kha na ma tho ba*). Unlike the four radical defeats (Tib. *pham pa bzhi*) of the prātimokṣa, which involve breaches of the monastic vows, the four radical defeats for bodhisattvas are considered here to be naturally negative because they go against the very nature of bodhicitta. Nevertheless, they are termed "radical defeats" because they destroy the foundation of the bodhisattva vow.

57. See note 55 above.

58. On his departure from Tibet, Guru Padmasambhava gave his disciples a number of different teachings, prayers, and so forth.

59. Mangalam (Skt.): "May it be auspicious."

60. Jamyang Lodrö Gyamtso is one of the names of Shechen Gyaltsap Pema Gyurme Namgyal (1871–1926).

Glossary

aggregates, *see* **five aggregates.**

arhat (Skt.), Tib. *dgra bcom pa,* a worthy one. The Tibetan translation of this term means "one who has vanquished the enemy" (the enemy being defilements). Arhats are practitioners of the **Basic Vehicle** (that is, **listeners** or **solitary realizers**) who have attained the cessation of suffering, that is, **nirvāṇa**, but not the perfect buddhahood of the **Great Vehicle**.

Basic Vehicle, Tib. *theg dman,* Skt. *hīnayāna.* Literally, "Lesser Vehicle" (in relation to the Mahāyāna, or Great Vehicle): the vehicle of the **listeners** and **solitary realizers** that leads to the state of **arhat**.

bodhicitta (Skt.), Tib. *byang chub kyi sems.* Literally, "the mind of enlightenment." On the relative level, it is the wish to attain buddhahood for the sake of all beings, as well as the practice of the path of love, compassion, the six transcendent perfections, and so forth, necessary for achieving that goal; on the ultimate level, it is the direct insight into the ultimate nature.

bodhisattva (Skt.), Tib. *byang chub sems dpa'.* A follower of the **Great Vehicle** whose aim is perfect enlightenment for all beings. One who has taken the vow of bodhicitta and practices the six transcendent perfections.

Cittamātrin (Skt.), Tib. *sems tsam pa.* Also called Yogācārin. A follower of the Mind-Only philosophical school of the **Great Vehicle**, based on the teachings of Asaṅga.

complete purity, Tib. *rnam par byang ba,* Skt. *vyavadāna,* the opposite of **total affliction**, equivalent to liberation and **nirvāṇa**, and associated with the truth of the path and the truth of cessation.

defilements, Tib. *nyon mongs pa,* Skt. *kleśa.* Mental factors or afflictive emotions that influence thoughts and actions and produce suffering. For the five principal defilements, *see* **five poisons**.

dharmakāya (Skt.), Tib. *chos sku.* Literally, "Dharma body": the emptiness aspect of buddhahood; also translated as "body of truth," "absolute dimension."

Diamond Vehicle, Tib. *rdo rje'i theg pa,* Skt. *vajrayāna.* Also called Secret Mantrayāna. A branch of the **Great Vehicle** that uses the special techniques of the tantras, based on the realization of the diamond-like nature of the mind and taking the result as the path, to pursue the path of enlightenment for all beings more rapidly.

five aggregates, Tib. *phung po lnga,* Skt. *pañcaskandha.* The five psychophysical components into which a person can be analyzed and that together produce the illusion of a self. They are form, feeling, perception, conditioning factors, and consciousness.

five paths, Tib. *lam lnga.* The paths of accumulation, joining, seeing, meditation, and no more learning. These comprise five different sections of the path to enlightenment, which follow one after the other.

five poisons, Tib. *dug lnga.* The five defilements, which are bewilderment, attachment, hatred, pride, and jealousy.

Four Noble Truths, Tib. *'phags pa'i bden pa bzhi,* Skt. *caturāryasatya.* The truth of suffering, the truth of the origin of suffering, the truth of cessation, and the truth of the path. These constitute the foundation of Buddha Śākyamuni's doctrine, the first teaching that he gave (at Sarnath near Varanasi) after attaining enlightenment.

Great Vehicle, Tib. *theg pa chen po,* Skt. *mahāyāna.* The vehicle of the bodhisattvas, referred to as "great" because it leads to perfect buddhahood for the sake of all beings.

listener, Tib. *nyan thos,* Skt. *śrāvaka.* A follower of the **Basic Vehicle** whose goal is to attain liberation for himself or herself as an **arhat**.

Mādhyamikas (Skt.), Tib. *dbu ma pa*, the followers of Nāgārjuna who adhere to the Madhyamaka, the Middle Way that avoids the extremes of existence and nonexistence.

maṇḍala (Skt.), Tib. *dkyil 'khor*. Literally, "center and circumference." The universe with the palace of the deity at the center, as visualized in tantric practice.

mundane, Tib. *'jig rten pa*. The opposite of supramundane, anything that does not transcend saṃsāra. Translations of this term as "ordinary" or "worldly" can be misleading since non-Buddhist meditators who have mastered the four dhyānas (but without being liberated from saṃsāra) and who have immense powers of concentration, magical powers, and so forth, cannot really be called "ordinary," nor are they necessarily worldly in the sense of being materialistically minded and interested only in the present world.

nirvāṇa (Skt.), Tib. *mya ngan las 'das pa*. Literally, "beyond suffering" or "the transcendence of misery." While this can be loosely understood as the goal of Buddhist practice, the opposite of **saṃsāra** or cyclic existence, it is important to realize that the term is understood differently by the different vehicles: the nirvāṇa of the **Basic Vehicle**, the peace of cessation that an arhat attains, is very different from a buddha's "nondwelling" nirvāṇa, the state of perfect enlightenment that transcends both saṃsāra and nirvāṇa.

path of accumulation, Tib. *tshogs lam*. The first of the **five paths**, according to the Bodhisattva Vehicle. On this path, one accumulates the causes that will make it possible to proceed toward enlightenment.

path of meditation, Tib. *sgom lam*. The fourth of the **five paths**, during which a bodhisattva traverses the remaining nine of the **ten levels**.

path of seeing, Tib. *mthong lam*. The third of the **five paths**, the stage at which a bodhisattva in meditation gains a genuine experience of emptiness and attains the first of the **ten levels**.

prātimokṣa (Skt.), Tib. *so sor thar pa*. Literally, "individual liberation": the collective term for the different forms of Buddhist ordination and their respective vows, as laid down in the **Vinaya**.

Samantabhadra (Skt.), Tib. Kun tu bzang po, "Universal Good." (1) The original buddha (Skt. Adibuddha), the source of the lineage of the tantra transmissions of the Nyingma school; he who has never fallen into delusion, the absolute-body buddha, represented as a naked figure, deep blue like the sky, in union with Samantabhadrī, as a symbol of awareness-emptiness, the pure, ultimate nature, ever present and unobstructed; (2) the bodhisattva Samantabhadra, one of the eight principal bodhisattva disciples of Buddha Śākyamuni, renowned for the way in which, through the power of his concentration, he miraculously multiplied the offerings he made.

Samantabhadrī (Skt.), Tib. Kun tu bzang mo. The consort of Samantabhadra.

samaya (Skt.), Tib. *dam tshig*. Literally, "promise." Sacred links between the teacher and disciple, and also between disciples, in the **Diamond Vehicle**. The Sanskrit word *samaya* can mean agreement, engagement, convention, precept, boundary, and so forth. Although there are many detailed obligations, the most essential samaya is to consider the teacher's body, speech, and mind as pure.

saṃsāra (Skt.), Tib. *'khor ba*. Literally, "wheel." Cyclic existence, the endless round of birth, death, and rebirth in which beings suffer as result of their actions and defilements.

self, Tib. *bdag*, Skt. *ātman*. In Buddhist philosophy, the term "self" is used to denote the mistaken notion of a permanent, single, and independent entity, whether applied to a personal sense of "I" or a divine creator.

senses-and-fields, Tib. *skye mched*, Skt. *āyatana*. Also called sense bases, sources of perception, and so on. The twelve āyatanas comprise the six sense organs and the six sense objects. Together, they give rise to the six sense consciousnesses.

solitary realizer, Tib. *rang sangs rgyas*, Skt. *pratyekabuddha*. The term applied to followers of the **Basic Vehicle** who attain liberation (the cessation of suffering) on their own, without the help of a spiritual teacher. Although some solitary realizers with sharp intellects remain alone "like rhinoceroses," others with dull minds need to stay in large groups, "like flocks of parrots." Solitary realizers' practice consists, in particular, of meditation on the twelve links of dependent arising.

sublime being, Tib. *'phags pa,* Skt. *ārya.* Also, "noble being." Usually someone who has attained the **path of seeing** in the **Great Vehicle**, a **bodhisattva** on one of the ten bodhisattva levels; in the vehicles of the listeners and solitary realizers, a stream-enterer, once-returner, non-returner, or **arhat**.

sugata (Skt.), Tib. *bde bar gshegs pa.* Literally, "one who has gone to bliss." An epithet of a buddha.

tathāgata (Skt.), Tib. *de bzhin gshegs pa,* "one who has gone to thusness." A buddha; one who has reached or realized thusness, the ultimate reality. Also, one who is "thus come," a buddha in the body of manifestation (*nirmaṇakāya*) who has appeared in the world to benefit beings.

ten levels, Tib. *sa bcu,* Skt. *daśabhūmi.* The ten stages of realization by which a sublime **bodhisattva** progresses toward enlightenment, beginning with the first level on the **path of seeing**. The nine other levels occur on the **path of meditation**. The eighth, ninth, and tenth levels are termed the three pure levels, or great levels.

ten nonvirtuous actions, Tib. *mi dge ba bcu,* Skt. *daśākuśala.* Killing, stealing, sexual misconduct, lying, divisive speech, harsh speech, meaningless chatter, covetousness, malice, and wrong view.

ten transcendent perfections, Tib. *pha rol tu phyin pa bcu,* Skt. *dāśapāramitā.* Transcendent generosity, discipline, patience, diligence, concentration, and wisdom, together with transcendent means, aspirational prayer, strength, and gnosis. Each of these ten is practiced predominantly on one of the ten bodhisattva levels—generosity on the first level, discipline on the second, and so forth. They are termed "transcendent" because their practice involves realization of the view of emptiness.

total affliction, Tib. *kun nas nyon mongs pa,* Skt. *saṃkleśa.* The opposite of complete purity, equivalent to **saṃsāra,** and associated with the truth of suffering and the truth of the origin.

vehicle of characteristics, Tib. *mtshan nyid theg pa,* Skt. *lakṣaṇayāna.* Also called the causal vehicle of characteristics. The vehicle that teaches the path as the cause for attaining enlightenment. It includes the vehicles of the **listeners, solitary realizers,** and **bodhisattvas** (that is, those bodhisattvas practicing the sūtra path and not that of the mantras). It is distinct from the resultant vehicle of the mantras, which takes the result (that is, enlightenment) as the path.

Vinaya (Skt.), Tib. *'dul ba.* Literally, "taming." The section of the Buddha's teaching that deals with discipline, and in particular with the vows of monastic ordination.

Yogācārin, see **Cittamātrin.**

Bibliography

Abbreviations

T Tōhoku catalog of the Kangyur and Tangyur

Ng Nyingma Gyubum, in the Tibetan and Himalayan Library, "Catalog of the Master Edition of the Collected Tantras of the Ancients," www.thlib.org/encyclopedias/literary/canons/ngb/catalog.php#cat=ng

Works Cited in the Text

Great Sovereign of Practices, the Victory over the Three Worlds (*'Jig rten gsum las rnam par rgyal ba rtog pa'i rgyal po chen po, Trailokyavijaya-mahākalparājā*). T482.

Guhyagarbha-tantra (*gSang ba'i snying po, Tantra of the Secret Essence*). T832, Ng 524 et seq.

Guhyasamāja-tantra (*gSang ba 'dus pa, Union of Secrets Tantra*). T442.

Kāśyapa Chapter (*'Od srung gis zhus pa'i mdo* [*sic*, probably *'Od srung gi le'u*], *Kāśyapaparivarta-sūtra*) in the *Ratnakūṭa*. T87.

Parinirvāṇa Sūtra (*Myang 'das* [*Yongs su mya ngan las 'das pa chen po'i mdo*], *Mahāparinirvāṇa-sūtra*). T119.

Sūtra of the Great Samaya (*Dam tshig chen po'i mdo*). A tantra. We have not been able to locate any extant work corresponding to this title that contains the passage quoted by the author, but it seems likely that the text quoted belongs to the *Guhyagarbha* literature.

Twenty Verses on the Vows of a Bodhisattva (*Byang chub sems dpa'i sdom pa nyi shu pa, Bodhisattva-saṃvara-viṃśaka*). A treatise by Candragomin. T4081.

Tibetan Commentaries on *A Garland of Views*

Jamgön Kongtrul Lodrö Taye ('Jam mgon kong sprul blo gros mtha' yas). *Man ngag lta ba'i phreng ba'i tshig don gyi 'grel zin mdor bsdus pa zab don pad tshal 'byed pa'i nyi 'od ces bya ba.*

Rongzom Paṇḍita (Rong zom pa chos kyi bzang po). *Man ngag lta phreng gi 'grel pa rong zom paṇḍita chen po chos kyi bzang pos mdzad pa.*

Tsultrim Zangpo (Tshul khrims bzang po). *Man ngag lta ba'i phreng ba'i dgongs don rtogs sla'i bsdus 'grel blo gros 'dab stong 'byed pa'i nyi snang zhes bya ba.*

English Language Sources

Dalton, Jacob. "A Crisis of Doxography: How Tibetans Organized Tantra during the 8th–12th Centuries." *Journal of the International Association of Buddhist Studies* 28, no. 1 (2005): 115–81.

Dudjom Rinpoche. *The Nyingma School of Tibetan Buddhism.* Translated by Gyurme Dorje and Matthew Kapstein. Boston: Wisdom Publications, 1991.

Kongtrul, Jamgön. *The Treasury of Knowledge: Book Six, Part Four: Systems of Buddhist Tantra.* Translated by Elio Guarisco and Ingrid McLeod. Ithaca, N.Y.: Snow Lion Publications, 2005.

———. *The Treasury of Knowledge: Book Six, Part Three: Frameworks of Buddhist Philosophy.* Translated by Elizabeth M. Callahan. Ithaca, N.Y.: Snow Lion Publications, 2007.

———. *The Treasury of Knowledge: Book Six, Parts One and Two: Indo-Tibetan Classical Learning and Buddhist Phenomenology.* Translated by Gyurme Dorje. Boston: Snow Lion, 2012.

Longchen Yeshe Dorje, Kangyur Rinpoche. *Treasury of Precious Qualities.* 2 bks. Translated by the Padmakara Translation Group. Boston: Shambhala Publications, 2010–13.

Shantarakshita. *The Adornment of the Middle Way*. Translated by the Padmakara Translation Group. Boston: Shambhala Publications, 2005.

Index

accomplishment
  of bodhisattvas, 49
  branch of, 19–21, 70, 82, 84
  in generation phase, 60–61
  great, 21, 70, 82–83, 84–85
  in Kriyātantra, 54
  of listeners and solitary realizers, 44–45, 47
  method of perfection and, 62–63
  in outer Yogatantra, 58
  through power of familiarization, 17, 71, 77, 87
  in Ubhayatantra, 56
accomplishment buddha, 60
accumulation of merit and wisdom, 15, 69–70, 71, 84
action seal of the activities (*karmamudrā*), 58
aggregates
  absence of self and, 5, 46, 51
  as five buddha families, 9, 11, 21, 64, 65, 83
  listeners' view of, 5, 43–44
  overcoming demon of, 84
Ākāśagarbha, 65
Akṣobhya, 65
all-illuminating concentration, 60
Amitābha, 65
Amogasiddhi, 65
Amṛtakuṇḍalin, 67
Anuttarayoga, 101n1
Anuyoga, xvii, 59, 61–63, 107n50. *See also* perfection phase
appearance
  basis of, 43–44, 103n13
  emptiness and, 49, 73–74
  illusory nature of, 65, 72–73
  relative truth and, 48–49
application, characteristic of, 17–19, 70, 76, 77, 78–79
approach, branch of, 19, 70, 81, 84
arhat, 45, 96
Atiyoga, xvii, 59, 107n50. *See also* Great Perfection
attributes
  absence of, 84, 87, 107n49
  maṇḍala of wisdoms and, 87
Avalokiteśvara, 66
awareness
  bodhicitta as nature of, 61, 62, 65
  direct realization and, 75–76
  as illusory gnosis, 15, 73–74
  pure self-cognizing, 52

birth, natural buddha and, 60
blessing, realization through, 15, 70, 74, 78
bliss
  transforming all into, 56
  wisdom of supreme, 21, 83–84

defilement
nine degrees of, 44–45, 103n15
overcoming demon of, 84
deity practice
four branches and, 19–21, 81–84
in Kriyātantra, 7, 51, 52–53, 54
method of perfection and, 61–62
in outer Yogatantra, 9, 57–58
in Ubhayatantra, 7, 55
deity/deities
generation of female, 19–21, 82, 84
knowledge of oneself as, 19, 81–82, 84
principle of, 52, 55
six, 52, 105n26
spontaneously present maṇḍala of, 59
two truths as nature of, 57, 61–62
dependent arising, 5, 45, 46–47, 104n18
dharma seal of speech (*dharmamudrā*), 58
dharmakāya, 87
Dhātvīśvarī, 11, 64, 65
Diamond Vehicle, 5, 7, 41, 50. *See also* Mantra Vehicle
direct realization, through perception, 17, 70, 75–76
discriminative wisdom, 75–76
dualistic clinging, purification of, 83–84

elements
arising of great mothers and, 21, 82
as five female buddhas, 11, 64, 65
listeners' view of, 5, 43–44
empowerment, 86
emptiness
Mādhyamikas' view of, 51, 105n25
space of mother and, 21, 82–83
union of appearance and, 49, 73–74
enlightened body, speech, and mind
adamantine nature of, 64
phenomena as nature of, 9, 17, 63–64, 77–78
realization by means of syllables and, 15, 73–74
as spontaneously present, 71
ultimate purpose and, 19, 79–80
See also buddhahood
entrance stage, 70
essential states, three, 52
eternalistic extremists
spiritual training of, 23–25, 90–91
views of, 3, 35, 36, 39–40, 43

familiarization
accomplishment through power of, 17, 71, 77, 87
characteristic of application and, 17, 77
entering the maṇḍala through, 21, 71, 85, 86
five buddha families
aggregates as, 9, 11, 64, 65

The Padmakara Translation Group

Translations into English

The Adornment of the Middle Way. Shantarakshita and Mipham Rinpoche. Boston: Shambhala Publications, 2005, 2010.

Counsels from My Heart. Dudjom Rinpoche. Boston: Shambhala Publications, 2001, 2003.

Enlightened Courage. Dilgo Khyentse Rinpoche. Dordogne: Editions Padmakara, 1992; Ithaca, N.Y.: Snow Lion Publications, 1994, 2006.

The Excellent Path of Enlightenment. Dilgo Khyentse. Dordogne: Editions Padmakara, 1987; Ithaca, N.Y.: Snow Lion Publications, 1996.

A Flash of Lightning in the Dark of Night. The Dalai Lama. Shambhala Publications, 1993. Republished as *For the Benefit of All Beings.* Boston: Shambhala Publications, 2009.

Food of Bodhisattvas. Shabkar Tsogdruk Rangdrol. Boston: Shambhala Publications, 2004.

A Guide to the Words of My Perfect Teacher. Khenpo Ngawang Pelzang. Translated with Dipamkara. Boston: Shambhala Publications, 2004.

The Heart of Compassion. Dilgo Khyentse. Boston: Shambhala Publications, 2007.

The Heart Treasure of the Enlightened Ones. Dilgo Khyentse and Patrul Rinpoche. Boston: Shambhala Publications, 1992.

The Hundred Verses of Advice. Dilgo Khyentse and Padampa Sangye. Boston: Shambhala Publications, 2005.

Introduction to the Middle Way. Chandrakirti and Mipham Rinpoche. Boston: Shambhala Publications, 2002, 2004.

Journey to Enlightenment. Matthieu Ricard. New York: Aperture Foundation, 1996.

Lady of the Lotus-Born. Gyalwa Changchub and Namkhai Nyingpo. Boston: Shambhala Publications, 1999, 2002.

The Life of Shabkar: The Autobiography of a Tibetan Yogin. Albany, N.Y.: SUNY Press, 1994; Ithaca, N.Y.: Snow Lion Publications, 2001.

Nagarjuna's Letter to a Friend. Longchen Yeshe Dorje, Kangyur Rinpoche. Ithaca, N.Y.: Snow Lion Publications, 2005.

The Nectar of Manjushri's Speech. Kunzang Pelden. Boston: Shambhala Publications, 2007, 2010.

The Root Stanzas on the Middle Way. Nagarjuna. Dordogne: Editions Padmakara, 2008.

A Torch Lighting the Way to Freedom. Dudjom Rinpoche, Jigdrel Yeshe Dorje. Boston: Shambhala Publications, 2011.

Treasury of Precious Qualities. Bk. 1. Longchen Yeshe Dorje, Kangyur Rinpoche. Boston: Shambhala Publications, 2001. Revised version with root text by Jigme Lingpa, 2010.

Treasury of Precious Qualities. Bk. 2. Longchen Yeshe Dorje, Kangyur Rinpoche. Boston: Shambhala Publications, 2013.

The Way of the Bodhisattva (Bodhicharyavatara). Shantideva. Boston: Shambhala Publications, 1997, 2006, 2008.

White Lotus. Jamgön Mipham. Boston: Shambhala Publications, 2007.

Wisdom: Two Buddhist Commentaries. Khenchen Kunzang Pelden and Minyak Kunzang Sonam. Dordogne: Editions Padmakara, 1993, 1999.

The Wish-Fulfilling Jewel. Dilgo Khyentse. Boston: Shambhala Publications, 1988.

The Words of My Perfect Teacher. Patrul Rinpoche. Sacred Literature Series of the International Sacred Literature Trust. New York: HarperCollins, 1994; 2nd ed. Lanham, Md.: AltaMira Press, 1998; Boston: Shambhala Publications, 1998; New Haven, Conn.: Yale University Press, 2010.

Zurchungpa's Testament. Zurchungpa and Dilgo Khyentse. Ithaca, N.Y.: Snow Lion Publications, 2006.

Ekajaṭī

Rāhula

Dorje Lekpa

Shenpa Marnak